To Marion,

Best wishes

Mark Wadley

Thank you for your
wonderful hospitality

ABOUT THE AUTHOR

Born in Edinburgh in 1958, Mark Wardlaw was educated at Edinburgh Academy and studied medicine at Dundee University, encouraged by his father, Elliot Wardlaw who had never fulfilled his own dream of becoming a Doctor.

Initially Mark studied Pathology with a view to being a Forensic Pathologist but, missing patient contact, he decided on General Practice and trained in Manchester.

After working twenty four years as a General Practitioner in Birmingham and Liverpool, he retired with his wife Jane to the rugged beauty of north Cornwall in 2012.

COMMEMORATING
THE CENTENNIAL ANNIVERSARY
BATTLE OF MESSINES
FLANDERS BELGUM
JUNE 7-14 1917

© Mark Wardlaw
First Published in UK 2017 by MMSANDJWARDLAW.CO.UK
Registered as a Limited Company
Paperback edition 2017

A CIP catalogue record is available from the British Library

ISBN 978-1-5262-0643-5

Cover & Page Design by TLC Holdings
Printed & bound on 100% recycled paper by Premier Print Group

www.brokenbymessines.co.uk

BROKEN BY MESSINES
IN WWI
The Grandparents I Never Knew

Mark M S Wardlaw

This book is dedicated to my late Father
He was always my inspiration
Without him there would be no story

THIS IS A LOVE STORY OF ROMANCE AND TRAGEDY
ADVENTURE AND OPPORTUNITY
SET JUST BEFORE AND DURING THE TURMOIL
OF THE FIRST WORLD WAR

CONTENTS

The Ornate Wooden Box which contained this Story

PREFACE

The Wooden Box

It was not long after my parents died in Leith, Edinburgh that the house was cleared. In a cupboard I discovered an ornate wooden box which had belonged to my father's mother Catherine Bell Hay (known as Kate). The box contained many letters, photographs and other items which she had kept during her time in New Zealand: 1912-1917. Most of these letters were from Peter Hutchinson Wardlaw – my grandfather. My father Elliot Wardlaw had never said much about his father, so I knew almost nothing about Peter.

Here was a chance in these letters to find out about him. I did not know then, but I was about to unearth a fascinating story set at a time of immense opportunity crushed by savage war.

The letters are dated from 1910 to 1917. I have presented these letters in chronological order and in italic script. I have tried to fill in where possible between letters with relevant information to help the story along. I have also included other letters from friends and family which were present in the box. These help to add background to the story along with photographs and other items. I have included the few scraps of information that I can remember from my father when he was alive.

This box contained a wonderful story and I am sure Kate had kept it safe so that a hundred years later their story could be told.

Just like other people living their lives and making plans, Peter and Kate would never have thought there would be a world war. If this happened to any of us, how would we cope?

Family photo February 1889 (PC1B)
Kate is the baby aged 4 months, Father Gilbert 37, Mother Ann 35, Brother Gilbert
11 and Sister Ann 5

1

BACKGROUND

Catherine Bell Hay was born in Alloa, Central Scotland on 9 November 1888 *(PC1A & PC1B)*. She was the third of four surviving children to Gilbert and Annie Hay.

Kate's Birth Certificate born 9 November 1888 (PC1A)

The Hays were a long established family in Alloa. Gilbert was a carpenter. By the time Catherine (known as Kate) was eighteen both her parents were dead and she was working for Mrs Lean as a domestic servant in the posh side of Glasgow – Montgomerie Drive in Kelvinside *(PC1C)*. She was also nanny to Mrs Lean's two young children *(PC1D)*.

Statistics from census data collected in 1911 indicate that 40% of the female workforce in Britain was involved in some form of personal domestic service *(Ref 75)*.

Many of Kate's friends had also left Alloa. With the excellent rail network in Britain young people were able to get jobs away from home and visit distant places.

28 Montgomerie Drive Kelvinside (PC1C)

Mrs Lean's young family, Kate was their Nanny (PC1D)

Kate's address book survives. She was an avid letter writer who kept in touch with friends and family. Unfortunately few of these letters survive, however there are several cards sent from Linda, one of Kate's friends from school days. She knew Kate as "Kitty"; young women just keeping in touch, 'social media' 100 years ago, no different from now with boys and happy times their main interests *(PC1E-G)*.

Linda worked as a domestic servant in a house attached to the Brewery in Thornton-Le-Moore, Yorkshire. These cards are addressed to Miss Kitty Hay either at Montgomery Drive, Glasgow, or to the holiday address in Biggar, Scottish Borders.

May 26th 1909.
Dearest Kitty,
When are you going to visit me? I have been looking for a letter for over a week. Hope you recognise the last House on this view. Sorry the photographer has omitted the seat.
Best love. Linda.

August 30th 1909.
Dearest Kitty,
Do you recognise this view? Can you fancy you hear the boys whistling. Are you coming out Kate? Down at the Brewery Gate. Happy days then dear. Shall we hope for them again though not the work?
Love Linda.

July 10th 1910.
My Dear Kitty,
Thanks for letter and enclosed. I did like the photos. I am sure you haven't altered a wee bit. I have put an X on Lou's and Jack's house. Write a P.C. and let me know how you like this. I will not write a letter till I hear from you. With fond love from Linda.

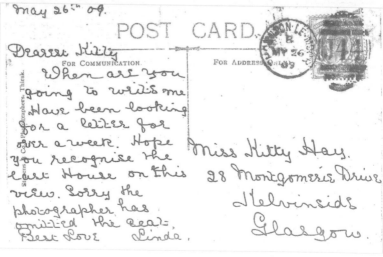

Card from Linda, Kate's friend from schooldays 26 May 1909 (PC1E)

Card dated 10 July 1910 (PC1F)

"Social Media" card dated 30 August 1909 (PC1G)

There is also a card from Jean Kemp, Kate's cousin, dated July 1911 and sent to Kate in Biggar.

Dear Kate,
Your arrangements will suit me although will try and leave about 3 o'clock. I have made it all right about that boy. Never mind the... [I am unable to read what is written. It may be derogatory]
Jean. (PC1H)

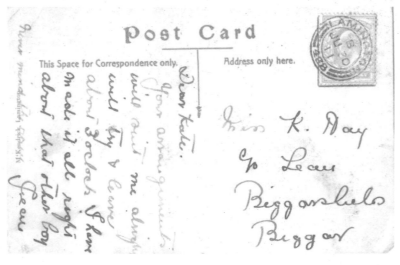

Card from Kate's cousin Jean (PC1H)

Other happy times shared with friends were weddings *(PC1I)*.

Kate spent most of her summer holidays in Biggar. She would have been with her mistress Mrs Lean at Mount Pleasant on domestic duties and looking after the children *(PC1J)*. It was here that she met Peter on the Biggar Road in the autumn of 1910.

With
Mr. and Mrs. Robt. K. Robertson's
Compliments.

CRAIGLEA,
COWDENBEATH.   20TH DECEMBER, 1911.

Henrietta Harris Thomson

Henrietta's wedding invitation to Kate 20 December 1911 (PC1I)

Kate on a picnic near Biggar summer holidays with Mrs Lean and family (PC1J)

Around Christmas time Peter asked if he could meet up with Kate in Glasgow. In the New Year of 1911 they were dating. The two earliest pictures of Peter and Kate are from 1911 *(PC1K & PC1L)*.

Peter Hutchinson Wardlaw
1911 aged 22 (PC1K)

Kate Bell Hay
1911 aged 22 (PC1L)

[Christmas time 1910. Undated letter.] *21 Grange Rd. Alloa.*
Dear Kate,
Pardon one for not sending a card as I had not your address and only received it when I arrived home. However I wish you a merry and happy Christmas. I will be in Glasgow on Monday first 26th; should you happen to be in the city any time about five o'clock, I will be at Queen's Street Station at that time and would like very much to have the pleasure of meeting you again. Hoping this finds you in good health and again wishing you all the good wishes of the Season.
Yours sincerely P.H. Wardlaw.

Peter Hutchinson Wardlaw was born in 1889. He was the second of four sons to James and Mary Wardlaw. James was the manager of a glass bottle making plant in Alloa and Mary was a dressmaker *(Ref 62)*. Alloa was a small close knit community so the Hays and the Wardlaws would have been aware of each other.

Alloa lies on the north bank of the River Forth in the Central Lowlands of Scotland. Alloa had grown to be a substantial port in the 18th and 19th centuries where goods from Glasgow were exported to mainland Europe. Although as a port it was in decline by 1900, it was still an industrial town with coal mining, weaving, glass making and brewing *(Ref 63)*.

The next letter is undated but talks of the Coronation. When the Edwardian era came to an end, George V acceded to the throne on 6 May 1910 and was crowned King at Westminster Abbey on 22 June 1911. It is therefore likely that this letter was written in February or March 1911.

Dearest Kate,
It was very good of you indeed to write me and you confined to bed. I hope this will find you better and back to your old form. Curiously enough you got my letter in bed and I also got yours but I was only enjoying a "long lie" that morning. The few days at our disposal seem to have slipped away very quick and tomorrow will be the usual busy out and in trials of every day work. You were saying you could do a weekend of your holidays down the Clyde, but Kate the Clyde is alright but a much better time could be spent at Blackpool, or the Isle of Man. Have you ever been to either of them? I am waiting my mother's arrival to see how her options will work out.

The boys and I are thinking of going to Blackpool at Easter, but I scarcely like the idea of going with her on holiday. However I do like Blackpool and have spent a good many holidays there. It will be all holidays now for a change until August has passed.

They are all waiting for letters from me at 21 Grange, but it will do them good to wait a while. My mother always says so and so is to expect a letter from you. There is some talk of the Whitsun holidays being postponed owing to the Coronation but I don't think such is the case. Although if it should be I will (if I arrange to do so) have mine at that time.

We are still having dull dismal weather just as I think the sunny days are not far away. No doubt you will be thinking they cannot come quick enough but they say such things are only sent to try us, and I sincerely hope you are not letting old troubles bother you again. I will now close thanking you for your letter and hoping you are well again.

Yours very sincerely Peter

The above letter is sent from 98 Claremont Road Rugby. Peter had moved to this address some time in 1911. This was the home of Mr Bob Duffus *(PC1M)*, his wife, and two daughters Margaret and Annie *(PC1N)*. Mrs Duffus and Peter's mother were good friends. Mr Duffus was an engineer. He had moved to Rugby to work at BTH. It was he who had helped Peter to get a job in this company. The British Thomson-Houston Co Ltd at that time was a massive electrical and mechanical engineering company *(Refs 3 & 66)*, a dream job for an ambitious young man.

The boys in the letter are Peter's three brothers; John born 1888, James 1891 and Alick 1896 *(Ref 62)*. The family home in Alloa was 21 Grange Road.

Bob Duffus (PC1M)

Mrs Duffus, Margaret and Annie (PC1N)

This letter would indicate that Peter did not always take the time to write regularly to his family and friends. However he did find the time to write to Kate.

The early dates of Peter and Kate's courtship are sketchy; few letters survive from this time. However other letters reflect back on the happy times they shared together in 1911, for example Peter's letter of 13 August 1912 reads *"you cycled to Carstairs and saw me on the way back"*. Also the letter of 6 July 1913; when Peter recalls how a boat trip on the Trent in Nottingham reminded him of his trip on the River Forth with Kate. His letter of 27 July 1913 refers to him stopping at the Railway Station in Symington two years previously. He was on his way to see Kate in Biggar. She was looking after her mistress and two children who were on holiday there.

I do not know what Kate's old troubles were that Peter refers to; perhaps it was to do with both her parents dying when she was in her teens.

At some stage Kate had developed a fascination with New Zealand, and it was her intention to go to the Colony, to work there and visit its beautiful scenery. Sometime in 1911 Kate became aware of a suitable job in New Zealand. There is no information as to how she found out about this. It is possible that adverts had been placed in Scottish papers to attract appropriate candidates. The post was for an Assistant Matron at The Girls' High School, Napier, New Zealand. This school had opened in 1884; courses included English, French, Latin, German, Drawing and Callisthenics (exercises to develop strength and grace), a significant number of girls boarded *(Ref 5)*.

Kate and her cousin Jean Kemp applied and were accepted to work at the girls' school. Kate would be looking after the needs of the girls who boarded. I do not know what Jean was going to do, perhaps domestic duties. What an adventure for two young ladies on the other side of the world.

Kate was given excellent references from the family she worked for in Glasgow and senior figures in Alloa who had known her since birth. These are shown below and I presume she would have sent off similar references with her application. The headmistress at Napier Girls' School was called Miss Greig *(PC10)*.

The reference letters are the following.

Nov 1911. 28 Montgomerie Drive. Glasgow.
Kate Hay has been with me as a domestic servant for more than four years. I have found her an excellent worker, honest and obliging. She has had a good deal of experience in my nursery with young children, and also in general house work. I can thoroughly recommend her in every

way. It is with regret that I part with her on her decision to go abroad, and she carries with her my best wishes for her future. .
Frances Beatrice Lean.

Feb 10th 1912. 13 Park Circus Glasgow
This is to certify that I have known Miss Hay since she was a child. Also her parents who were a very much respected family in Alloa Scotland. I can thoroughly recommend Miss Hay as a good and trustworthy girl and hope she may meet with people who will take an interest in her and I feel sure she will do her very best for them.
I am yours respectfully.
Mary. B. Cochrane.

10/2/12 John Dawson, Mayburn Alloa.
I have much pleasure in testifying as to the character of Miss Kate Hay. I have known her personally from childhood, and have found her to be always sincere, kindly and most diligent in every respect and most willing to help anyone to the best of her abilities. I have every confidence in recommending her, and anyone regarding her services, in my opinion, will find her most capable and willing to please, and will also perform every duty entrusted to her most faithfully. I wish Miss Hay "God speed", and trust she will be successful in the new land she is going to.
John Dawson. Senior Elder. Chalmers UF Church. Alloa
[This referee was a relative of Nellie, Kate's sister-in-law, who was married to Kate's older brother].

Feb 10th 1912. Grange Manor. Alloa.
It gives me much pleasure to testify to the true approachable character of Miss Hay. I have known her all her days. She had excellent parents and enjoyed a fine home backing. I am sure she will in any position present herself courteous, faithful, and obliging.
J. Wilson Harper .DD

On 11 December 1911 Kate purchased third class passage to travel from London to Napier on the SS Remuera sailing on 15 February 1912 *(PC1P & PC1Q).*

The cost was £2 and 16 shillings, around £300 in today's money *(Ref 50).* I presume food and drink would have been an additional cost.

Most of these references were written after she purchased her ticket so she was already going, taking the letters of reference with her.

In January 1912 Kate visited Peter in Rugby. She travelled by train. On her way back to Glasgow she visited Peter's Mother in Alloa. This would have been a pleasant friendly gesture getting acquainted with her boyfriend's mother.

Miss Greig, Head Mistress
Napier Girls' High School,
New Zealand (PC1O)

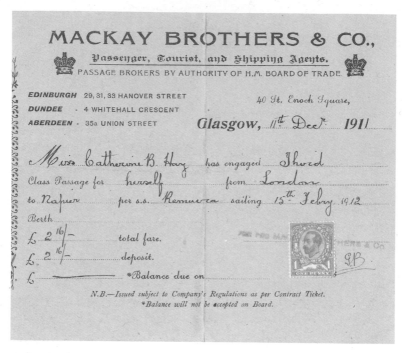

Kate's ticket to New Zealand (PC1P)

Kate and Jean had tickets for the second voyage of the SS Remuera sailing from London on 15 February 1912 (PC1Q)

2

ROMANCE

9/2/12, 98 Claremont Road
Dear Kate,
No words can tell how delighted I was to have your very nice letter today,
for which I thank you and also the telegram. It is real good of you Kate
dear to send a telegram as I was anxious about your arrival in Alloa.
I am sorry to hear that you had so many [train] changes, and were so
much upset between Preston and Glasgow, but I think it was rising so
early for the long journey. In the first place Kate dear I am delighted and
appreciate all your thanks, and I may say the best thanks I owe you for
your visit South which has passed as a dream, and I can only look back
with pleasure to the few happy days we spent together. Every hour of the
busy day Kate dear it makes me think of you and your departure, and
I should like you to say you will trust me with the trust and love I have
for you. I cannot think that distance can ever stand between us, when
happiness of the highest degree comes to both of us when we are in one
another's company.

I may say Kate dear that it is such thoughts that always surround me
when I think of you and makes all the hardships and troubles worth
enduring. I am glad to think I will meet you again so soon, although to
say a little Good-bye, but cheer up Kate dear we will make this only a
little incident in our lives.

If you will pardon me introducing work again. I am glad to tell you I
have got the advance I told you about, and a little more than that. In
the middle of this afternoon I was offered charge over all the Outsides
Patterns and Castings for the BTH, which means looking over some 60
firms all over England which do work for us. However I have got to

consider what I think of it, and I may say I am pleased at the offer, but Bob is in a way about it and doesn't know how he will go along if I am away. I am considering both our interests, for he has been a real good Boss and friend to me and he will think affairs rather peculiar if we cannot discuss them together.

I would seldom be in Rugby and would be daily travelling about from one firm to another. However big and responsible it is I have no fear. I would give it a good trial. As you remark about your head being in a whirl, mine is scarcely like that, but a different idea comes forward every minute. However there is no hurry and the subject will be fully discussed during the next week and as I seem to be a "lucky person" I will be transferred to the "Commercial" under yon Person whose lamp I lit the Sunday night I was with you. Kate dear you seem to have brought me good luck ever since I have been interested in you; I seem to have had a great many opportunities, and have been encouraged by your kindness. Need I say I shouldn't like anything known just now, as I have not said a word to the Grange People although I am writing home tonight.

I thank you very much for visiting my Mother and my Cousin. I am sure they would be more than pleased to see you. Now Kate dear I am looking forward to your letter telling me the time you will travel and what docks etc. you will sail from. I have already arranged about being off next Thursday. Bob and Roxburgh were off all day yesterday and I did have a day of it to 8.30 at night.

I trust you will think lightly about the long oh's and laments you will be getting from most of the Alloa Folks for thinking of it as they talk of it won't do you any good. Be of the cheer as you usually are and of the future not of the past. I do wish I were talking to you Kate dear instead of writing as my thoughts are ever of you. I have been writing in the chair you used to sit on at the window, with Marg and Annie wanting me to bring Auntie Kate back again, and I wish I could satisfy their wish (PC2A). Goodnight once again Kate dear and a pleasant day in Glasgow tomorrow is my most sincere wish, with the love from all at 98.

Yours very sincerely Peter.

Kate's chair next to the window
Margaret, Annie and Mrs D
(PC2A)

Peter considered himself to be lucky since he had met Kate. He had been offered an excellent promotion at BTH. This involved travelling to sixty different suppliers all over Britain. However he does not know if he should take the job and intended to discuss it with Bob Duffus. He had received an advance from the bank, even more than he had originally thought; it is not clear at this stage what this loan would be for.

His lighting of a lamp is interesting, definitely metaphorical, but possibly it did happen. He would have had to ask the Street Lamp Lighter if he could light the lamp; "a flame for Kate". At that time Street lighting was being modernised. By 1912 many of the old gas lamps had been replaced with electric lights. The old gas lamps were connected to a gas supply which came from the gasification of coal, manufactured in numerous gas works throughout urbanised Britain. There was no "natural gas" then. The gas was lit around a mantle which had been improved in 1890 by the Austrian scientist and inventor Carl Auer Von Welsbach. This improvement resulted in a brighter light, which became the standard street light throughout Europe. It was gradually replaced by electric lighting in the 1900's. Many of these lights were made by Mazda in the BTH factories *(Refs 3 & 52)*.

Peter and Kate must have had a very nice time together in Rugby. He is aware of the mixed opinions back in Alloa regarding Kate's decision to leave for New Zealand. Some of her friends and family would be worried about her leaving a good job and sailing away to the unknown, others would admire her courage.

Kate would be going to Glasgow to say goodbye to her former employer in Kelvinside. She was also Nanny to Mrs Lean's young children *(PC2B & PC2C)*. This would be quite heart wrenching. The brother and sister that she had looked after for almost five years had grown to know her well and she would have loved them dearly.

Equally traumatic would be Kate's departure from Alloa as she said goodbye to family and friends. She was staying with her older brother Gilbert, his wife Nellie *(PC2D)* and their two little girls; getting her things ready for New Zealand. Gilbert had been her rock after their parents died. She would miss him dearly.

*Kate the Nanny
(PC2B & PC2C)*

*Nellie, Kate's sister-in-law,
married to her brother Gilbert
(PC2D)*

*Envelope containing Peter's letter to
Kate. She was at her brother's home
in Alloa getting ready to depart for
New Zealand (PC2E)*

13 February 1912. [Letter from Peter to Kate, who was at her brother's address;] *21 Queen St, Alloa, Clackmannanshire (PC2E)*
My Dear Kate,
Many thanks for your two nice letters I received today at midday. I am indeed sorry to hear that you had such misfortunes while at Glasgow, and no doubt you would be a bit excited at the time. Well Kate Dear I heartily thank you for all the nice passages in your letter, and I am glad to know you have the faith in me that I have in you. My thoughts are with you every minute Kate and only wish I could be a little nearer you at such a time as this when I know you need such a friend. My one desire in life Kate Dear will be a desire common to both of us, and I was delighted to hear you say you would be true to me while you are away, and I will say likewise Kate Dear that I will be true to you. At times Kate Dear I feel as though somebody was guiding me and my thoughts run deep to know of you. I am glad I will be meeting you on Friday and if I don't meet you when you arrive in London, I will meet you at Fenchurch Street Station. However Kate Dear when you tell me your time of arrival I will endeavour to be there.

I have accepted the Position I spoke of. I will start on Monday. At first it will be a big change, but I will do my utmost Kate Dear to give it a fair trial. It is very good of you to think of me and my work, and I am looking forward to the day if we are both spared when you shall return and we will face our troubles and pleasures together.

Now Kate Dear excuse this short letter as I am writing in the office and haven't had a night off since you left. I am enclosing two Photos which I hope will reach you safely, and also your tickets from which I have taken all particulars of Friday. Thanking you Kate Dear from the Bottom of my heart for your nice letter and our early meeting. Goodnight Kate Dear and a safe journey is my sincere wish.

With the best of love from Peter

It is my impression that it was Kate's ambition to travel to New Zealand, to work there and to experience the beautiful scenery and wonders that she had heard about. Also I believe it was her intention to come back to Britain at some stage in the not too distant future to be with Peter. This was only to be a temporary separation. They were in love *(PC2F)*.

Peter and Kate together 1912. The only picture to survive (PC2F)

3

KATE DEPARTS FOR NEW ZEALAND

Kate and her cousin Jean Kemp travelled down to London. They used Mackay Brothers & Co, shipping agents for their luggage. Kate paid two shillings "for Cartage and Carriage Glasgow to London", she was not taking much, just one package is recorded. The receipt indicates that the SS Remuera was to sail on 16 February 1912 *(PC3A)*. This ship was ordered by the New Zealand shipping company in 1910 and was built by W Denny at Dumbarton, Scotland. She was launched on 31 May 1911 and delivered several months later in September 1911. She was triple-screwed and driven by triple expansion steam engines.

Luggage ticket for one item Glasgow to London
(PC3A)

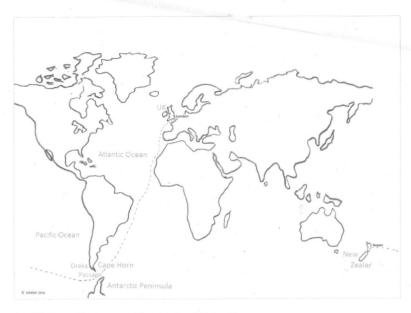

World Map - Kate's trip to New Zealand (Map 1)

She was made specifically for the New Zealand to Britain route via Cape Horn *(Map1)*, then in July 1916 via the Panama Canal which opened in August 1914. Her very early career was relatively uneventful apart from a collision with the steamer Niobe off The Lizard, Cornwall in 1912 on her second voyage *(Ref 4)*. Kate must have mentioned this damage to my Father and that repairs were carried out in Tenerife as I remember him telling me about this.

Peter and Kate met up in London before the SS Remuera started its long voyage. It would have been an emotional departure. In a letter written later Peter would recall watching the ship, *"I saw you sail away"*. They had kept their romance alive between Glasgow and Rugby – some three hundred miles. Soon Kate would be thousands of miles away in New Zealand. They had both stated their intention to be true to one another. Would their love survive such a distance?

How long would they be separated?

On the passenger liner SS Remuera, Kate and Jean made many friends with fellow travellers; most of them were probably setting out for a new life. There is a group photo of several young people with a caption stating *"best party on the SS Remuera 1912" (PC3B)*. Some would become close friends in New Zealand, in particular Will Berry as shown in his photo of 1912 *(PC3C)*. He addresses Kate as *"sister"*, but saw Jean as a future wife!

"Best party on the SS Remuera"1912, above (PC3B)

Will Berry, left, met Kate on the SS Remuera March 1912 (PC3C)

Conditions would have been very cramped in third class passage with six to a berth. At some stage on her long voyage Kate became very ill with Rheumatic fever. This was to have lasting consequences and shorten her life with disabling valvular heart disease; again this is information from my Father. In the pre-penicillin era infections now treated easily could have long lasting effects. It is interesting that there was an outbreak of Scarlet fever aboard the SS Remuera in 1913 which resulted in one death *(Ref 4)*. Both Rheumatic fever and Scarlet fever are caused by the Streptococcus – so readily transmitted in such cramped conditions.

The sea voyage would have been an amazing experience as they sailed down to Cape Horn where the Atlantic meets the Pacific. This body of water is known as Drake Passage and lies between Cape Horn, Chile and the South Shetland Islands of Antarctica. Today modern powerful ships equipped with the latest technology including stabilisers take two days to travel through the 830 km channel. One hundred years ago it would have taken a lot longer.

Many sailors consider it to be the most dangerous shipping passage in the world, with violent unpredictable weather and massive waves up to 14 metres high. The reason it is so rough is due to the volume of water rushing through this channel: 600 times the flow of the Amazon River. It is an area renowned for ship wrecks; very scary for those on the SS Remuera in 1912 *(Ref 78)*. Alternatively they could have been lucky sailing on "a mill pond" in the southern hemisphere's summer sunshine.

Kate and Jean arrived in New Zealand after a voyage of six to eight weeks covering some 11,000 miles and started working at the Girls' School in Napier probably in April 1912.

There are no letters in my possession from Peter between Kate's arrival in New Zealand and this letter dated 30 June 1912. There must have been some correspondence because he states *"I told you last time"* regarding his forthcoming trip to Canada.

30.6.12. 98, Claremont Road. Rugby
My Dear Kate,
Now that I have a minute or two to spare, I will answer your welcome letters of this week. How pleased I am dear to know how well you are getting on and that you are settled down. I am sure you have had a lot to do and were beginning to get tired of it. No doubt you will be looking for this letter of mine to know a little more about me going off to Canada. However Kate dear I will dwell more on that subject after I have discussed the New Zealand talk.

I was telling Bob the other day about you learning horse riding (PC3D), and all the time he was saying you had surely got into a good place. He bids me say he had a funny little accident last week with your pipe. Having finished smoking it he slipped it into his pocket—Result in a few minutes a blaze; he will be more careful next time. I was saying a man come to his time of life ought to have known better. And Oh the pipe (PC3E) - for he is eternally talking of its nice dark colour and all the rest of it. No doubt Kate dear it is really a good one and he dearly loves it.

It is good to know that Jean is near you, so as to have a few little talks together and share your joys and sorrows. It is more than kind of you Kate dear to think of me so often, and I am sure my imagination and my thoughts have carried me further since you went away - than ever they did before. How I should love to have a few hours with you, and in my thoughts if I could only picture you in New Zealand as you do me in 98. It would make all the difference, if I could only see where you are with my own eyes, so as to cast aside any doubts about you being comfortable.

Since I wrote you last Kate dear I have been north in Glasgow and Edinburgh on business for the BTH and if you will pardon me just giving you the particulars of my running about since last Friday morning (Friday 21 June, *Ref 6*), *you will well see I have had little time at hand* (Map 2).

Kate enjoying horse riding in New Zealand, taken by Will Berry at Koro Koro Wellington (PC3D)

Bob Duffus, the pipe was a present from Kate (PC3E)

Rugby to Leicester
Leicester to Birmingham
Birmingham to Rugby
Rugby to Glasgow
Glasgow to Saltcoats
Saltcoats to Glasgow
Glasgow to Clydbank
Clydbank to Glasgow
Glasgow to Coatbridge
Coatbridge to Alloa
Alloa to Glasgow
Glasgow to Coatbridge
Coatbridge to Glasgow
Glasgow to Edinburgh
Edinburgh to Mussleburgh
Musselburgh to Edinburgh
Edinburgh to Rugby
Rugby to Manchester
Manchester to Rugby
Rugby to Birmingham
Birmingham to Leicester
Leicester to Rugby
Rugby to Derby
Derby to Repton
Repton to Derby
Derby to Nottingham
Nottingham to Rugby
Rugby to Leicester
Leicester to Rugby

Peter's 1500 mile round trip (Map 2)

I left Rugby a week past Friday at seven o'clock for Leicester at midday, from Leicester to Birmingham at five o'clock to Rugby, got home about seven, got ready for the 10.53 pm for Glasgow, accompanied by Mrs Duffus and children. They have got 8 weeks holidays. Landed at Glasgow Central at 7 o'clock on Saturday morning, had a rush to St. Enoch Station to catch the 7.10 for Saltcoats only catching the train as it left the

Station. Journeyed to Queen St and got the 7.35 for Clydebank arriving at my Uncles in time to wake them at 8.15 am. I had only a short time there, as I had a business appointment at 10 o'clock in Glasgow. I then went down to Coatbridge and returned in time to catch the 1.54 for Alloa. Arriving there I found the bold Jonnie like a soldier and a man all smiles about a yard long. Needless to say between meeting J. Dickson and one or two more at night it was 10.30 before there was any chance of bed and it really ended in retiring at one in the morning.

Sat gone. Sunday I had no intention of being at church, but I managed to Dirliton Gardens [this is where his older brother John's girlfriend Mary Morrison lived] *after midday, about two o'clock down comes John to go a walk, and along with the Grants (I don't think you would know them) we wandered towards the Dam* [The Gartmorn Dam had been constructed in the 18th Century to provide water power to operate the mines and other industries in Alloa - *Ref 63*] *after passing the brickworks, I began to "smell a rat", however there was a neat little Garden Party at the house of the Morrison's and I, one of the number, never knowing until I got there. They all seemed well pleased with themselves, but they didn't interest me as they were all strangers. That practically put the stopper on my week-end, and I hadn't been far. On Monday morning I intended going to Glasgow at 8.25, but I went at 7 to have a few old faces as company.*

I landed at Queens St. at 8.30 and I had two pairs of our Club Bowls at St Enoch Station which I brought with me to have altered by the maker. As I didn't have the address something seemed to say it was in Sauchiehall Street. Well Kate for a full hour I simply tried everybody with no success and I returned my bundle to the left luggage at 5 to 10, and I was catching the 10.13 for Coatbridge.

While at Queen Street the idea struck me to ring up Miss M. Clark

(PC3F) *and ask her to find out the address giving her the name of the firm, and saying they were Iron turners and Bowls makers* [she worked nearby]. *On ringing 3135 the person at the other end did get a fright, and in an instant she came to the Station. I had only five minutes to get the train, and our talk was short, she said she was anxious for your address which I gave her, then off in the train. When I came back to Glasgow another ring and I had all the particulars in a few minutes. As it was then ten minutes to six, she said "if I didn't mind" she would direct me to the place as she had just finished. Of course I was only too pleased to have a guide, after fulfilling the Bowling Club Business, I wanted to write a few letters to Rugby, and I was told I could write them at 166 Buchannan Street* [the place where she worked].

Mary Clarke a friend of Kate and Peter (PC3F)

After the post, something to eat was the next item and we had a few hours to spare before my 10.15 train. The Empire had to put up with our company for an hour and a half. Then Ta-ta and I was off to Alloa. John met me at the Station as I had a large bag of undesirables I didn't want to take to Canada.

It is needless to say of the attitudes of the Family, especially Jimmy who was down on his hands and knees. We retired as usual about one o'clock. After bidding them Goodbye, I went off to Edinburgh at 8.25 and was all day on business in Musselburgh, returning to Edinburgh in time to change at 9.05 pm for Rugby, arriving at 6 o'clock.

I went off to Manchester at 10 am and returned to Rugby at 2 am Thursday morning. Off to Birmingham first train, then crossed to Leicester arriving at 3 o'clock, played a Bowling Club Cup tie there from 3 to 6 and winning by 13 shots (31 to 18). Then I had business from 6 to 8, catching the 8 train arriving Rugby 9 pm. On Friday forenoon off to Derby, then to Repton and back to Derby. By that time it was about ten o'clock, the last train gone. I went to Nottingham, changed to another railway and got the midnight to Rugby, arrived at 3 o'clock Saturday morning.

I went to the Works at 9 am came home in time for the Leicester train at 2 o'clock, Bob and I missed it, while all the Bowling team caught it. However we got the 2.30 and had a "hansome" [cab]. It was all chat for the rain was simply tumbling down. We got a serious thrashing. Finished too late for the 8 o'clock train, managed to catch the 11 o'clock, and we got home after 12 o'clock. Excuse the news but it is a bit too much. I covered about 1500 miles in that time.

Now Kate dear after plodding through that you will be ready for my Canadian news, as near as I can say I will sail in 5 weeks' time. I want to have a week with Bob, if I can manage before that. The Old Folk at Alloa seem to say little and the Old Chap, said anything I wanted it was there for the asking. I am going to Manchester tomorrow and I will see the exact time that the boat sails. I think I told you last time, that I am going to meet the captain of the ship I will travel with, through some people I do business with, who are related to the Captain.

The ship only takes first [class] passengers and I think I will be all right. I am busy getting all my odds and ends together. The most of them being information of one kind or another I intend taking. Poor Mrs Duffus, she is a real good sort. She was crying one day before she left, about me going away. However I will make a point of seeing her again before I go, as I intend going north (if time permits) again.

Now Kate dear when you first told me of your going off to New Zealand I was in many different thoughts and I didn't know exactly what to think of it. But now it is reverse and I expect you will be in the same position as myself, and everybody keeps on telling me about the good position I am leaving, however Kate dear it is a good position and a risky one. One simple slip might cost hundreds of pounds, however I have done my best and have been exceptionally fortunate so far, but the chance that has been put before me is a big one, an opportunity which only comes once, and to many, never. I know too well what is in front of me, but I am out to give it a trial and a severe one at that; and can only hope for the best.

The experience alone will make me able to take up a higher position here, should I have occasion to come back. All that lies in the glorious unknown.

Now Kate dear before wandering away any further, I think you and I know one another well enough now, and it is my desire that we should become engaged (PC3G). I first thought it would have been more suitable when you were going away, but I thought you had so much to do and time so short, that it would be much better if you had been where you now are, the country where you so longed to travel, now being fulfilled, you have a better chance of thinking matters over. How I do wish Kate dear that I was talking to you now, instead of writing. It seems unfortunate that all our exchange of words should be conveyed, without our meeting in person.

Many an hour Kate dear when I am travelling around I think of how you are doing, and I am glad to think of the trust and love we have in one another, and hope for our being spared to meet at the opportune time. My Kate dear, I trust you have the confidence in me, and that anything

I can do in the slightest way for you, that I may have the opportunity. I feel as though I have always been so busy and short of time, not to have given you the attention I should and if I could only have written as often as I should have liked, I for one would have been more satisfied. However I thank you Kate dear for the many good wishes you have sent me, and I am proud to think of your ambition and also proud of having been favoured with the thoughts of yours when we are so far apart.

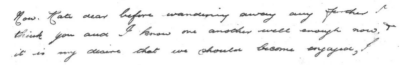

Peter's proposal of engagement (PC3G)

How I will long for your reply to my letter. My imagination often makes me think that I should have known you longer than I have, for there is no doubt everybody needs someone to share his thoughts or her thoughts; and it is with pleasure I look back on the days when I made your acquaintance.

It is now beginning to get late and I should like to post this tonight, if possible, by the way I had to talk with Kate McEwan, and she was asking kindly of you. And also numerous more, and I said you were doing well. Kate McEwan don't change much, the same Kate, almost since I first knew her. I will now close with the best of wishes from all at 98, and the best of love that words can contain, and a Goodnight from,

Your loving Peter.

Peter was glad to hear that Kate was well and settling into her new position. He was clearly impressed that she was horse riding; an activity not so readily available back home. He may not have been aware that Kate, Jean and Will Berry shared this interest. [Photo *PC3D* of Kate on Horseback was taken by Will at Koro Koro; beautiful

Maori countryside near to Wellington. Riding is also mentioned in letters written later, so the mutual interest continued].

Peter was amused about Bob's pipe catching fire in his pocket. It had been a present from Kate to Bob. He was also pleased that Jean was with her for support.

He mentioned his travels; both business and pleasure; going to the Empire after meeting up with Mary Clark, a mutual friend who helped him out in Glasgow.

The Empire Theatre was built in 1897. It was an immense building four storeys high which held 2150 people. It was very ornate copying the French and Italian Renaissance style. The building was faced with beautiful red sandstone from Dumfriesshire. The main theatre entrance was 31 Sauchiehall Street with shops next door and the luxurious Empire Bar at the corner with West Nile Street - under this was a lounge area for smoking, and over the bar were large billiard rooms. All varieties of entertainment were performed in this theatre, until it was replaced by Empire House in 1971 *(Ref 2)*: Kate would have known this part of Glasgow well - the heart of socialising in the city - and would have felt some nostalgia as she read Peter's letter, she may even have felt home sick.

Peter intended to go on business to Canada in August 1912 travelling first class. He saw that his situation was similar to Kate's when she set sail for the unknown of New Zealand. They were kindred spirits.

He was getting his things together and was planning to meet the captain of the ship that would take him across the Atlantic. He was not sure how long he would be in Canada or if it would be a more permanent move. He was going to visit the Cargill Company which had been started in 1865 by William Wallace Cargill. They had built a grain warehouse in Conover, Iowa at the end of the McGregor Western Railway. This helped farmers move their grain to market *(Ref 36)*. From his letter Peter clearly saw this as an opportunity not to be missed. Unfortunately there are no letters that relate directly to his time in Canada.

4

ENGAGEMENT

Peter states in in his letter of 30 June 1912 *"that it is my desire that we should become engaged…"* What a shock such a request would have been for Kate thousands of miles away and Peter possibly embarking on a new life in Canada! However he is confident that they will meet again and that she will agree to the engagement.

Other letters were being sent to Kate in New Zealand. She received a letter from her niece Lalla aged six, Gilbert's daughter, dated 18 July 1912, and addressed from 21 Queen Street, Alloa:

Dear Aunt Kate,
Thank you very much for the nice little present you sent me. I have put it in the Bank. The School closed last Friday for seven weeks. I got a nice prize for class work. It is called Blackie's Children's Annual.
Mama is sending you the paper, and you will see my name in the list. We are going to Carnoustie for a fortnight.

[The letter is finished by her mother Nellie] *Poor Lalla has asked me to finish her letter. It's too hot for writing she says. She just wants to tell you that Daddy gave her a lovely dolly for doing so well at school, and she had it at school for the Dolly Song.*

XXXX from your own Lalla.

Blackie's Children's Annuals were first produced in 1904 and continued until 1940. The Publishers came up with the idea of taking the best of the year's stories, articles, and illustrations and putting them together as an "annual" released late in the year for Christmas sales *(Ref 51)*. This concept continues today. The annual would have been an excellent prize for a studious little girl who would one day be a headmistress herself.

Kate kept in touch with friends and family in Scotland and with Mrs Duffus in Rugby. She would have been aware of home events from newspapers sent to her. One letter states that she received a weekly paper from Alloa.

Gilbert was ten years older than his sister Kate, he was born in 1878. He married his childhood sweetheart Nellie Anderson. Nellie had given him a ring engraved as a statement to this effect. This ring was in the ornate wooden box which contained the letters. There are scratches and gauges on it presumably from his work as a carpenter following in his father's footsteps. They had two daughters Lalla born in 1906 and Nan in 1909 *(PC4A and B)*.

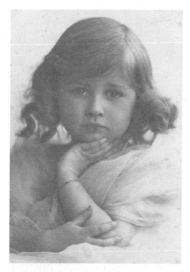 

Lalla Hay born 1906 Kate's Niece (PC4A)

Nan Hay born 1909 Lalla's sister (PC4B)

In August Peter was back in Alloa on holiday at his parent's house.

8/8/12. 21 Grange Road.
My Dear Kate,
Holidays, holidays, holidays, oh yes it is holidays spent in Alloa. I daresay
Kate Dear you have had some.

The early part of the week I went north to Bob's home, where I met Mrs
D and the family, looking much the better from their stay in the country.
The weather has been very bad and you can scarcely say, to be safe, that
there will be any better prospects tomorrow.

How I wish Kate dear that you had been in the vicinity of Alloa, just so
as we could have an evening or two together once again. It seems a long
time now since I saw you sail away and it is when I am off duty, such
as I am now, that I feel so lonely. However we can only trust our time
will come round, in due course. My father and mother are going off to
Troon tomorrow morning and I am going to Glasgow to see them right at
St Enoch Station. I expect John will be through at midday and we will
spend the rest of the day together [Troon is a seaside resort on the west
coast of Ayrshire; now famous for its links golf course].

I am going back to Rugby on Monday and I expect my marching orders
for Canada will be awaiting me. Oh that glorious unknown future
Kate, everybody says I shouldn't do this or I won't go so and so, giving
all their advice free of charge. But never mind Kate dear I will meet you
somewhere all being spared and well, if not in England, New Zealand,
or Canada it will be somewhere else, all depends on the move of the hoard
at the time.

However between us we seem to be having our share of roaming around.
I often wonder what will happen next. It seems so long before we can

hear from one another and to think before we can have a reply it takes 3 months, 4 in a year, what oh that's covering ground isn't it. Now Kate dear I hope you won't think (think twice if you please) me forward as I thought of sending your engagement ring before waiting your reply to my letter, but it will be another 6 or 7 weeks before I get that reply and dear knows I may be in Cargill by that time. I thought dear when in Glasgow tomorrow of selecting one to my own fancy and trust to it suiting your taste. I would much rather that you do the choosing, but under the circumstances we cannot have all we should like. On the other hand Kate dear I have faith in you to agree with my idea. Did you say great minds think alike?

I seem to have little news to give you about Alloa and it is just a case of meeting this one and that one having a talk, passing one and the same over again. Grand isn't it and supposing I don't go away I don't intend spending another holiday here in a hurry, unless I happen to be in Glasgow on business and ran across. I have had as much Alloa this time to do me for a long time to come.

Often I try to picture you Kate dear one time enjoying yourself not caring whether it snows or blows, the next time sitting pondering over old times perhaps better left alone, but many's a night I think of your hurried visit to Rugby and the happy evenings we had together but these few evenings have had to last us a long time now Kate, haven't they however the clock keeps going round and time little boys like me were in bed. Hoping this finds you dear, fit and well and got over your troubles in getting hardened into the winter of your new climate.

With all the love to your dear self, Kate and a happy Goodnight from your Loving Peter.

Peter had informed Kate that he was not going to wait for her reply to his request to be engaged but would go ahead and purchase an engagement ring in Glasgow and send it to her in New Zealand! He was very confident indeed.

It would appear that he experienced some negative comments and lack of enthusiasm in Alloa for his intended trip to Canada. He was also missing Kate and longed for more *"happy evenings"* with her.

August 13th 1912.
My Dear Kate,
As I told you in my last letter I went to Glasgow and stayed the weekend there, meeting Bob Duffus on the Monday. We both went to Troon and had two hours with the old folks. They are very comfortable and enjoying themselves.

After I saw Bob off in the Perth train I went to Samuel's in Argyl Street and bought your ring and treated myself to a new non-magnetic watch guaranteed to suit all climates. I sincerely hope Kate dear that the selection I have made will suit you. It was packed, registered and posted last night by Samuel's, who will be responsible for delivery at your address in Napier. To make no mistake you might let me know dear when it arrives, that all is in order. It has 3 blue stones, the centre one being a little larger than the side ones, and I hold a receipt to be sent back whenever I hear from you. The size was the only thing I wasn't exactly sure about and after a few comparisons I think it will fit you alright, if not I don't suppose you will have any trouble getting a jeweller to alter it a little. However I hope you won't need to go to that trouble dear.

I go back to Rugby tonight from Glasgow and will join the crowd from Perthshire at Carlisle. I was just thinking now, how last year at this time you cycled to Carstairs and saw me on the way back. It was really too far for you dear and more than kind of you to attempt it, but never mind we can smile over it now, although it was no smiling for you on the way home that night. [Biggar is eleven miles from Carstairs. At this Junction the train is split, one part for Glasgow, the other for Edinburgh. On the return journey one half waits for the other before moving south together].

I will have to bid you goodbye once again dear, for by the time I get packed up and ready for the road it will be train time, hoping you are well and happy.

With fondest love from your loving Peter

This engagement ring has survived (see front cover). It was present in the bottom of the wooden box that contained the letters. Until I read the letters I had no idea of its significance. It is a gold ring with three blue sapphires and two small diamonds in between. Peter had sent it 11,000 miles to reach Kate in New Zealand. I think he must have loved her very much.

31st August 1912. 98 Claremont Road Rugby.
My Dear Kate,

For the life of me I cannot understand what has become of all your letters. There was a spell when I didn't hear from you for an age and the letters I have received since, all read the same that you have not received any letters from me.

Well Kate Dear you will have a load lying somewhere for I am sure there is something wrong with the mails. I received a postcard, a letter and something else enquiring if I was dead or what. Well I am not quite but getting on towards that way. But putting all joking aside dear it seems strange that you haven't had my letters for I am sure I have written half as many again as you dear.

All this goes on when we less deserve and need it, and our patience does get tested to some tune. I hope you are not down hearted dear and keeping up your spirits. It is nice to hear Jean is beside you. You will feel more at home, and soon have the place your own.

I am still doing away as usual and no doubt you will be wondering if Canada is still to the fore. Well Kate dear I have all the particulars of the sailings and have had a letter from across the Atlantic and no doubt I am going to a good place, and they are all rather anxious at Home about me going away.

I had John [Peter's older brother] *down for 8 days (PC4C & D), but unfortunately I was as usual away nearly all the time. We have been nearly flooded out all over the Midlands, with such rain storms; we never knew the likes before. In one town about 10,000 were homeless, while round the outskirts of Rugby all the fields were like the sea but calm of course.*

Now Kate dear I will stop as the dinner is on the table and there is a lot to do today. Trusting you are well and happy. With the fondest love to your dear self.

Your loving Peter.

Peter was concerned that their ability to communicate was being compromised and was causing some distress to them both.

He sailed to Canada in September and returned at Christmas. The next letter is dated 16 April 1913 and was sent from 98 Claremont Road Rugby. Perhaps there were letters from Canada to Kate but I

Peter moved to Rugby in 1911 and lived with Bob Duffus, his wife and children Margaret and Annie photo from 1912 when John Wardlaw visited (PC4C)

The Duffus family with Peter and his brother John in a horse drawn carriage (PC4D)

did not find any. It would have been interesting to know what Peter experienced doing business for the BTH with the Cargill Company in Canada.

There is no mention directly stating that Kate said yes to getting engaged, however the tone of Peter's letters changes. He starts with

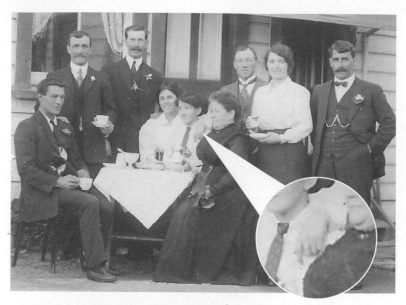

Staff at the Girls' High School Napier Kate next to her maid Jean standing the large lady is the Matron Miss Lily (PC4E) [Inset, the engagement ring (PC4F)]

"My Dearest" or *"My Own Dear Kate"*. He also finishes the letters *"with fondest love, your loving Peter"*. So I would conclude she had responded in the affirmative.

Having looked very closely under a magnifying glass, in two group photos where her left hand is visible, they do show her wearing an engagement ring *(PC4E, F, G & H)*. There is however no mention of this ring in any other letters; whether it fitted her finger or if she liked it!

16/4/13. 98 Claremont Road Rugby.
My Own Dear Kate,

How pleased I was to have your nice letter tonight. I have let my correspondence get slightly behind and I have just written home, where I

Jean, Kate and staff Girls' High School Napier Kate is wearing her engagement ring (PC4G) [Inset, Kate's left hand showing her engagement ring (PC4H)]

feel sure my Mother will think I am dead or something.

You seem to be having very warm weather dear. I do hope by the time this reaches you, it will be more like what the Old Country was, and let's hope when the heat does turn away; it won't be as cold and raw as we are having here.

By your letter dear you were saying your maid (PC4I) is M.F.C.'s image [this is Mary Clarke - *PC3F* - a friend, mentioned in an earlier letter who met up with Peter in Glasgow]. *That reminds me I had a letter from her shortly after I returned at Christmas and I have never acknowledged it yet, however patience and perseverance I may manage some time.*

I trust Kate dear you had a good holiday at Easter. Holidays are welcome aren't they, when one feels tired out and I feel sure Jean and yourself will be ready for all the half days during the summer.

As for things at Rugby they are much as usual, as busy as ever, and for myself dear I don't quite remember if I told you but I have a good offer to go to Glasgow. However I haven't come to any decision yet and I am only telling "in advance" as I don't want them at home even to know until later.

Margaret is much better since her operation and seems to be gaining every day, while Annie not a word, she simply beats everything. I doubt I will have to stop for post time as a matter of fact I am writing after being late at the works, hoping this finds you dear as usual well and happy.

With fondest love. Your loving Peter.

Kate's maid and staff The Girls' High School Napier (PC41)

Kate and Jean with male friends "to Miss Kate Hay from Jim in Remembrance" the photo is torn; did something or someone upset Kate? (PC4J)

A page from Kate's little black book Peter's address in Rugby (PC4K)

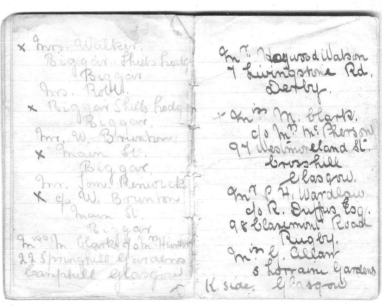

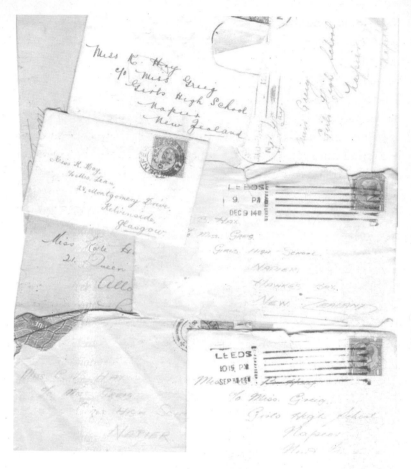

Envelopes addressed to Kate (PC4L)

Invitation sent to Kate to attend her friend Ann's wedding 1913 (PC4M)

Kate would appear to be doing very well in her position at the school as Assistant Matron and now had a maid to help her. She had made many friends; some of her male friends may have admired her and wished for more *(PC4J)*. She was not an unattractive woman. Kate's little black book *(PC4K)* which was in the wooden box contained the names and addresses of people in New Zealand and Australia as well as friends and family in Britain. She liked to keep in touch through letters and cards *(PC4L)*. Among these is an invitation sent to Kate to attend her friend Ann's wedding in England on 14 June 1913 *(PC4M)*.

Ann McLeod married 14 June 1913 (PC4N)

Her friends back home were getting married.

Later in 1913 Kate received a card from her friend Ann wishing her a Merry Christmas and a Happy New Year. It is signed Ann McLeod; her married name *(PC4N)*. She had finally got her man and was settling down. How long would Kate have to wait now that she was engaged?

5

INVENTION AND DEVELOPING A BUSINESS

June 25th 1913. 98 Claremont Road, Rugby.
My Dearest Kate,

I have missed your usual letter this week and I am again a week late in writing, however dear by your last letter you were starting on your holidays and I do trust you had a good time, as I have no doubt it is well deserved.

Mrs Duffus starts her holiday's tomorrow night going straight to Alloa for about a week. Then for a run further north until August. Now was the time dear as Bob used to say to keep house for both of us and what a jolly time we could have. Quite a change wouldn't it dear to have your company for a while. What a lot we would have to talk about, however all that is to be looked forward to.

We are still doing away in the old way here. Bob and I have just made a more complete sowing machine that I told you about before. [This is the first letter that I came across to mention this, so there were others that are missing]. *We are going out into the country to sow a whole field for so far everything points to be in our favour, however I will write you later and tell you all about it.*

I suppose you will see by the writing I am catching the post, as I generally do, on Sunday. Except last Sunday I was working for ourselves [Bob and Peter] *and of course how time flies.*

I am now off to the post and also to make arrangements for Mrs D having a comfortable journey tomorrow.

Trusting this finds you dear as usual happy and well.

With fondest love, your loving Peter.

It is possible that when Peter was on business in Canada seeing the machines for processing grain he became aware that mechanical methods of sowing seeds could be improved. He and Bob had been working on this since his return from Canada and were now trying out their prototype in the fields outside Rugby.

Perhaps it was to finance this project that Peter had obtained a bank loan the previous year.

June 29th 1913. 98 Claremont Road.
My Dearest Kate,
It is now Sunday afternoon and a glorious one, the sunshine being just nice. I received the paper you sent alright. It was very interesting indeed, and I am sure there seems to be plenty of scope in the colony.

I am all alone in my glory this weekend. Mrs D and the children have gone north and are at present in Alloa, while Bob is at Blackpool for the weekend. We are dining across the street at Mrs Muston, same as last year, where we have things just as at home.

Yesterday was a great day in Rugby, being the hospital fete, favoured with glorious weather. The success beat all previous efforts. I only managed to get there at night as we had a bowling match in the afternoon, which we just managed to pull off by one shot [I think we refers to Bob and himself].

Five weeks today will be our holidays, so far I haven't quite made up my mind where I shall go, but I do not anticipate going north, (as things may develop somewhat) during the next few weeks, and the (spare time) may come in very handy indeed.

I think I told you dear that we were unsuccessful in our attempt to take over some business premises in the neighbourhood, since then we have been negotiating to purchase another site and should have news in a week or so.

I was pleased indeed Kate dear to read in your last letter, of the increase you have received. Not only do I feel it is well merited, but also nice to think your labours are being appreciated. That alone is a big item which commands respect.

Saturday next I expect to be at Leicester playing in the rink Championship of the Midlands, where we will have to be in our best behaviour to succeed. However we will soon know all about it, as a week seems like a day now.

Trusting this finds you dear in the best of spirits.

With fondest love, from your loving Peter.

So for Peter and Bob the sowing machine project was progressing well and they were looking to purchase a site to manufacture their invention. They both appear to enjoy playing bowls, and found the time to take part in competitions. However as the project grew there would be little time for anything else.

6th July 1913. 98 Claremont Road Rugby.
My Dearest Kate,

It is now Sunday and raining at that. We have had a lot of warm weather and the rain is quite welcome.

Mrs Duffus and the family are still not at Grange Road and from reports seem to be having a good time, saying nothing of Bob and I being here on our own. However we are managing away as usual while Mrs Muston always attends to her duties at meal times.

Last week I had a lot of running about; Tuesday night I had a grand sail in a pleasure boat on the Trent while at Nottingham. I was wishing dear you had been there. It made me think of the old days on the Forth, but the Trent is so nice and pleasant especially in the evening, the water being ever so clear.

Yesterday I was playing Bowls at Leicester with 3 others, including Mr Roxburgh in the Midland Counties Championships and after an exciting game we returned winners by 2 shots. This puts us into the Final, played on 19th July, and all being well we should make a good show.

As for our little business transactions dear we cannot get away as fast as we should like, owing to the trouble in purchasing land. However during the next week we should know something of the site we are now interested in. However it means starting at the foundation and building complete, which means additional time, whereas the site we just missed included buildings complete.

Our seed sowing machine will be in action this week, sowing a complete field. Bob and I have just returned from the farmer's place and he has examined our first attempt and is highly delighted with the results.

I have not had your usual letter this week dear, but I cannot say too much as you are like Mrs Duffus, you get the bulk of the writing to do. However

I trust this finds you in the usual good spirits,

With fondest love, your loving Peter.

Unfortunately none of Mrs Duffus' letters written to Kate survive. They may have been helpful in providing information about events later in this story.

July 15th 1913. 98 Claremont Road Rugby.
My Dearest Kate,

Many thanks for your ever welcome letter of Sunday morning. I am glad to hear you had a good rest during your holidays, as holidays to such as us are always well earned.

No doubt you would see in the Alloa paper (you have talked of having it each week) of Alick's [Peter's youngest brother] *success at the secondary school, having carried the premier honours including the "Dux Medal", need I say Kate dear, I was as proud as though it had been myself and the folks at 21 Grange Road are more than pleased. He has done well indeed and it is nice to think so many of his labours have not been in vain.*

Possibly you may have had a letter from Mrs D, who is now in Dunbar [this is where Mrs D's Aunt lived and looked after the Castle Hotel. Dunbar is a holiday resort on the east coast of Scotland], *having a good time and the kiddies as lively as ever. From what I can gather of the recent correspondence from Grange Road, the "Old Folks" may go to Aberdeen this year, and they are fully expecting my company. However Kate dear, I haven't made up my mind yet, whither to go north or not. "Plenty may happen between now and then". I am going to Leicester tomorrow with Mr Roxburgh, who is playing a Bowling match. While on Saturday we play at the same town in the Final of the Midland*

Championship and our expectations up to the present bid well in our favour.

Bob and I spent all day last Sunday out in the country at a Scotch Farmers place. We did have a good time - quite a change for two "Factory bound persons".

We have just had a nice heavy welcome shower dear, and didn't we need it not having had any rain for a long time. We were saying it would remain for another three weeks until the holidays.

I will bid you "Goodnight" once again dear, trusting you are as usual, happy and well,

With fondest love, from your loving "Peter".

There is no mention in letters that follow of how Peter faired in the final of the Bowling Championship on Saturday *(Ref 6)* 19 July 1913. By not mentioning it one can presume that he lost!

27th July 1913 98 Claremont Road Rugby
My Dearest Kate,
Bob and I are sitting in the back garden on this the last Sunday, for another term, of our 2 lonely Bachelor lives and we are fairly looking forward to going north on Friday night.

All being well I will go to Alloa, as usual on the Saturday morning, accompanied by Mr Roxburgh. We will stay over the weekend, and then go to Falkirk and Dollar to play bowling matches. On the Wednesday we go to Aberdeen to visit Mrs Duffus. Go on to Inverness, return.......
Friday morning, return to Aberdeen....... where I will meet the "Old Folks" who are going to stay at the Granite City [Aberdeen] for a week,

*after spending the weekend with them I will return direct to Rugby.
Quite a good run around don't you think dear, but I am sorry to say Kate
dear my Father is anything but well. I am afraid when I go north I will
have to make arrangements for him to have a complete rest, possibly at
Rugby, for a while and see how he improves.*

*In Mrs Duffus's absence we have had all the house done up and what a
surprise she will get for we don't intend to say a word until she returns.
I was pleased to have your letter of yesterday and I hope your new dress
dear will be as you are anticipating. The cold you speak of no doubt won't
last very long. I was pleased indeed to hear of the new sitting room which
has been placed at your disposal.*

*Well Kate, my dear, I will bid one "Goodnight" and a hearty Goodnight
at that, for had it been as two years ago, my journey would have been a
pleasant one, first stop Symington, however....... how sweet to recall the
thoughts....... reality.......* [The paper has been torn and is missing. It
ends in the usual way].

Your loving Peter.

Symington was the railway station for Biggar. This was where Kate
spent the summer looking after her Mistress Mrs Lean and her
children when they were on their holiday.

Just over a year had passed since Kate started work in the Girls' School.
She had been rewarded with a pay rise, a maid to help her and now
a sitting room at her disposal. This was praise and encouragement
indeed.

The next letter in date order is from Charles Newton Hutchinson
who is Linda's brother (Linda was Kate's friend from schooldays).

There are post cards from them to Kate as stated previously, received before she went to New Zealand). Charles was still interested in Kate.

The Hutchinsons' may have been distant relatives of Peter whose middle name was Hutchinson, his mother's maiden name passed down to her son; Scottish tradition.

August 30th 1913. C/o Mr H Stoddart, Jyalgum, Tweed River. NSW Australia.
My Dear Kate,

I wrote to you once before since I came to Australia, but I think it must of got lost, as I have had no reply. Linda writes to say she has had a letter from you and says you just have a PC from me (that was posted at Melbourne) and I wrote to you about a fortnight after the PC. So my dear Kate write to me if you receive this letter safe, then I will write you a nice letter back by return of post.

I have a good job here Kate and would like a partner like you Kate. Hoping you are keeping in good health as this leaves me well.

I am your sincere friend Charles.
Charles Newton Hutchinson XXXXXXXX

What a proposition? There is a post card *(PC5A)* from Charles who was visiting his sister Linda in Thornton-Le-Moor, North Yorkshire. It is dated 8 July 1908, five years previously. It is addressed to Miss K Hay c/o Mrs Lean Mount Pleasant, Biggar, Lanarkshire.

Dear Kate,
Spent the day at Redcar today Tuesday with the choir trip. Wish I could have seen you there. Had a ripping time.

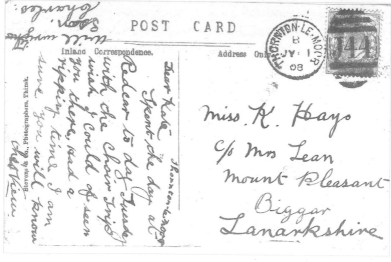

Postcard from Charles, Linda's brother sent to Kate in 1908
(PC5A)

I am sure you will know the view.
Will write soon. Charles.

It would appear that Charles had held a flame for Kate over many years and was not far away from her now that he was living in Australia. He had a good job and was interested in Kate as a partner! It would appear that Kate was not that interested in him. She was engaged to Peter. Was Charles not aware?

5th November 1913.
My Dearest Kate,
Many thanks for the three letters I have received written while you were on holiday.

It makes me look small dear when I think how often I have (neglected) to write, however Kate dear you know how much I have on hand and when I tell you this is now my fourth week in succession without a break, Sundays and all together, you will understand how my time flies.

I was pleased indeed to hear you had a good time, although perhaps rather quiet dear. What would I give for a quiet fortnight just now? In fact I am living in hope of having a chance of getting a weekend for a change somewhere, but I can never tell until the last minute. I am pleased to say dear our little venture here, has been so far successful, but what a lot to do. I feel sometimes it is too much. Then I think it is a chance in a lifetime I have got, and perhaps might be worse employed if I had less to do.

I had a letter from home. My father is slightly better and the Doctor says if he could recover his strength, he would be himself again. Fancy Kate he has had nearly four months now, however if he gets over it now time counts for but little.

I had a letter from Mrs D she says Margaret is gaining strength, but the Doctor never told them how really bad she was until she had recovered. Now Kate dear I am just getting ready for a busy night, it is now after six and I have as much as keep me going till midnight.

I will bid you good night dear, hoping you are as usual happy and well. Again many thanks for your ever welcome letters.

With fondest love. Your loving Peter.

The next two letters are from Lalla Hay, Kate's niece.

16th Nov 1913. 21 Queen St Alloa.
Dear Aunt Kate,

Thank you very much for the nice letter and cards you sent me, and I got a letter just shortly before it. Nan got one too. Nan is up at Mayburn and Dada has not very long gone up to meet her. [Nan is Lalla's little sister] *Nan goes to church now, but I have something else to tell you. Last Sunday she was at Sunday school and she is only four past in August. Mama and I are in the house and no one else is in, and we are both writing. You will likely be sleeping while I am writing this, but never mind; you will get the letter all the same.*

I am getting on nicely at school. I get my quarterly report soon. I hope there is something good in it. I am making a cushion slip at school, and before that I made a bachelor tea–cosy and now I am making one at home.

The shop windows are beginning to look pretty for Christmas. It is a long while till Xmas, but it will be Xmas when this reaches you so I will wish you a merry Xmas.

With lots of love from Nan and myself. XXXXXX

Wed 31st Dec 1913. Hogmanay.
My Dear Aunt Kate,

Thank you very much for the nice book and money you sent Nan and I. We have an awful lot of presents this year we can hardly count them. I got a great big Doll's bed from Santa Claus with a wire mattress. I am in my holidays. This is Hogmanay. We are all going to the Pavilion on Thursday, and Nan and I are going to a party on Saturday. This is awfully cold weather just now. You slip wherever you go and the snow has been on the ground since Saturday.

Nan is always wishing the geysers [the first footers of the New Year] *would come. Uncle Watson is in just now. Mama is down in the town just now.*

Two little girls in my class at school Jenny Westwater and Kathleen Rae have taken Diphtheria since the school closed.

I wish it was the time when you come home. As you often say in your letters, that you will play at all sorts of games and make doll's dresses.

With loads of kisses, from Lalla. XXXXXXXXXXXXXXXXXXXXXXXXXXXXX

This is the exact number of kisses at the end of the original letter. It would indicate that Lalla loved and missed her Aunt an awful lot. For Kate this letter from her niece would have emphasised what she was missing at home in Alloa.

Sadly a hundred years ago childhood illnesses that today are readily preventable with vaccination were often fatal. It is interesting that a German Scientist called Emil von Behring discovered the immunisation against Diphtheria in 1890 and received the Nobel Prize for his endeavour *(Ref 61)*. It was not until 1940 that Britain introduced a national immunisation campaign to eradicate this illness. Did the two little girls return for the spring term?

6

1914 PRE-WAR

January 1914. 98 Claremont Road, Rugby.
My Dearest Kate,

Time seems to simply fly away, just now and it will be spring again before we can really imagine it winter.

We have had Jimmie [the older of his younger brothers] *down for his New Year holidays, and although I didn't have much time to spend with him, Mrs Duffus fairly made him enjoy himself. Bob took him round the works on the Saturday morning. When I asked him what he thought of it I fancy he must have been speechless, at least he didn't say much.*

Annie has now gone to school, so Mrs D has quite a change at 98 now, while Bob says he must be getting old, all his family being at school (PC6A).

Things at home are not exactly what they might be, mainly of course through Father not being at all well, as I told you Kate dear. He has been laid up more or less for the past twelve months while the Bottle Works haven't seen him since last July. Poor soul he isn't well and I much doubt he will never get himself back again.

My Mother met the Doctor the other day, and I don't think she thought he was really so bad and of course she is worrying so. When I was last home I saw a severe change on him, and he told me himself that none of them knew what he had suffered. I said to do his best to carry out the Doctor's instructions, give him every opportunity and no doubt he would benefit by so doing. At the same time Kate dear I know full well

*Bob was getting old his daughters were
both at school 27 August 1914
(PC6A)*

*the hardened labours of his daily work, have now told their tale and it
remains for the best to be done in a quiet way.*

*Alick is now, as you know dear, at the University and likes it well and
says he has to work hard. That won't do him any harm, will it dear?
I only hope the success of his recent efforts will be long continued and
stepping stones to something higher.*

*You will have settled down again after the holidays, once more the
beginning of another year, which for you will add to past incidents of
your colonial life. Accept of my sincere wish Kate dear, that your efforts
will be even more fruitful in your daily toils, than they have in the past.*

*For myself dear last year has been full of adventures, with every week
being a new light to new opportunities, more and less advantageous. At
the present my headquarters are still at Shrewsbury, although I get to
Rugby occasionally and the time simply runs away. I have been more*

than obliged to Mrs Duffus of late for writing so much to you dear. I am glad to have the welcome news contained in your letters, to know you are happy and doing well.

With fondest love from, your loving Peter.

The next letter is from Will Berry *(PC3C)*. Kate and Jean had met Will on board the SS Remuera. The three of them had become close friends; they shared interests such as horse riding and visiting fascinating places. By January 1914 Will was in a relationship with Jean.

Will was a travelling salesman who worked for Ross & Glendining. This firm was started by two Scots - John Ross and Robert Glendining at the time of the New Zealand gold rush in the 1860's, it imported and distributed textiles. In the 1880's, it had its own manufacturing plant. More than ninety percent of profits between 1900 and 1914 came from warehousing and distribution of its textile products *(Ref 74)*.

21.1.14. C/O Ross & Glendining, Victoria Street, Wellington
Dear Sister Kate,

I must first thank you very much indeed for your cheering letter. I was downright glad to receive it, very pleased indeed to read that you arrived safely back, but I am afraid it was an awfully difficult journey for you.

I was thinking of you and that journey all day long and I can hardly express my regret at being unable to help you. I sincerely hope that by now things are running smoother for you and that you have regained your old cheery self. Both Jean and I miss you very much. Why on earth is Napier so far away? [It is 196 miles from Wellington].

Thanks very much Sister for your confidence in me. I can assure you I value your friendship, advice and confidence very much and I shall do my best to justify your opinion. Thanks ever so much for your enquiries and wishes re Mother. I am very pleased to say she is on the upward path, slow but sure. I will let you know any more news from time to time. Thanks very much for shortbread. I enjoyed it immensely, all the way from "Bonny Scotland".

Sorry to say we have struck bad lodgings. The appointments are alright but the food is cruel. We have therefore decided to shift at the end of this week, so please address letters to Ralph until I know better what I shall be doing.

Jean started at St. Joseph's on Monday, but I haven't heard how she has got on. I am going to see her tonight. I hope she is happy Sister Kate. I shall do my very best to make her so, and I do hope she will tell me if she is dissatisfied with anything.

Personally I think she would be wise to stick at Joseph's for a time even if dissatisfied, because it will be experience, and will enable her to take another place easily, by sticking it I mean for about 6 weeks. Do write her Kate and cheer her up.

Things are getting a little more settled here, and I hope soon to be able to report "all Happy".

Ernie is boarding with me and seems a little more sociable. Jean said that Miss Collette told her that he was offended, because I did not tell him anything about you two. That in my opinion is simply a pass off. In any case his methods did not, suggest any confidence, however all's well that ends well.

Candidly Sister we do miss the "Bach" at least I do, especially as I managed to find a decent cold and neuralgia last week, no convenience here, but it is nearly all gone now. [This would suggest that they made their own entertainment with musical evenings; singing and playing piano. Kate did play the piano well according to my father.]

As soon as Jean gets settled down, I hope to have some good trips with her. We should be happy, when a little time has passed and memory has faded. There is one thing, we both like each other, and that is a lot. By Jove what I have to thank you for Sister Kate! Someday I will repay it.

We had a trip out on the boat last Sunday over to Days Bay. Quite an exciting time after the disappointments of late. Came back at night and it was splendid. Still busy at the firm. I shall have to do one or two late nights, but it will soon be over.

Well Dear Sister I really must not worry you anymore this time. All send their best wishes here. I met Mrs Scroggs today, and she sends her love, also Helen and Miss Rouse.

Cheer up Sister; let me see you again soon. Very best wishes.
Your loving brother, Will.

Clearly something serious had happened in Napier which meant that Jean had moved to St Joseph's school in Wellington in a hurry. This "event" had put a strain on her relationship with Will. After all she was meant to be his girlfriend; however he was confident that they could work things out.

The next letter is written later the same day once Jean returned from work. She was not happy.

21.1.14. C/O Ross & Glendining, Victoria Street, Wellington.
My Dear Sister Kate,

Since writing my previous letter today I have seen Jean and that has altered the whole trend of events.

To commence with Jean is very unhappy in her place, and has not the least liking for her work. She cannot see the good of learning all the little things that seem necessary in her present situation.

Now while talking tonight she plainly showed that her heart and soul would prefer to be at the school at Napier. She was very happy there and it would take months to erase it. The shock of leaving so suddenly has been actually too much for her. It would have been much easier had she been prepared to leave.

Under those circumstances and after a real good talk, and think over it, I consider it would be much better for her to return to Napier if possible. There are objections certainly. One is the possibility of her meeting him, but I think if such was the case it would make very little difference, for if he is a gentleman he would respect her wishes. Secondly she considers it quite easy to keep out of his way for several weeks, and time will have healed a little by then.

The second is - is there anyone else to be a little afraid of in Napier, and if so is it possible to meet it? I think it is easily met, because she has acted in an honourable manner.

Thirdly or anyhow, there is myself to consider. Well I am quite confident to trust in her to remain true, and I know she has you to help her.

I am only willing to let her return because I know it is for her happiness.

I don't mind what she does as long as she is happy, because if she is happy so am I.

Now my Dear Sister I am aware that I have no right to ask you what I am going to do, but knowing you so well, allows me I hope a little more privilege than ordinary.

I want you if you will to help her in her troubles, to restrain her, for a time at least, from those temptations which her good naturedness leads her into, and to generally help her with that sound common-sense, and reliability which I know you possess.

You have done this all, I know for herself in the past, and now I want you to do it for me as well, if you are willing I know that things will turn out just as I desire.

Try and arrange with Miss Greig or Miss Lily, the excuse can be and a true one too, that she doesn't like parting with you, although I am here, I mentioned the latter because it might help. Wire me at R and G's if you have anything special to mention.

Well Dear Sister I don't think I can say more at present, but remember, if there comes a time that you want a friend, it does not matter what it is for, anything that it is possible to be done – financial, home, sickness or anything, let me know, and I will do it. Don't be afraid to speak on any subject. I am sensible and honourable on any point.

Well I must close. I am sorry for all the worry I am giving you, but I will repay it someday. For the present Au Revoir, Good luck and may God Bless you.

Your loving brother Will.

Will sounds quite determined to do his best for Jean. He is very fond of her, but are her feelings for him anything more than just friendship? He is grateful to Kate for introducing him to Jean, but now demands that she keeps Jean on the straight and narrow! Jean was missing her cousin and would like to be back with her in Napier. It is clear that something serious had happened which involved another man resulting in her leaving her job in a hurry. She is prepared to "front it out" with the "gentleman". However she needs Kate to ask the Head Mistress for her job back.

Next is a letter from Peter, who is aware that Jean had left Napier, but not that she wants to come back.

8/3/14, 98, Claremont Road, Rugby
My Dearest Kate,
Thanks awfully for your remembrances while on holiday. It gives me pleasure indeed to know you are having, what you equally deserve, a real good time, after a strenuous term. Your ambition Kate dear of my company would have been to my delight.

On the subject you opened regarding Jean, I was very interested of course, unfortunately not able to give any suggestions. But on the other hand, I feel convinced both of you should be best able to judge and I sincerely trust the decision will ultimately be the correct one, as I have no doubt it will. You will miss her company Kate dear, but still that can be an occasional circumstance against a continual one; quite easy, isn't it.

When I received something like ten articles with one mail, I had the feeling Kate that my part had been neglected, however I know full well you understand the conditions here and all opportunities are being made the most of. From the following you will see the temperament of our attentions of late and the results.

*To cut matters short, we are starting business on our own, in company
with two other gentlemen in the district. The works are being built
now, in a small town 7 miles east of Rugby. Everything is now definitely
decided regarding the action of each individual. Bob is going to manage
it practically while I was going to look after the Commercial interests
however the Company we are at present employed with would not release
me, so I am staying on and have got a very good position, with plenty to
do of course. With one thing and another weeks are now resembling days.
However Kate dear I know we have your good wishes that our efforts will
be duly rewarded.*

*The above address will soon be a thing of the past. All afternoon yesterday
we were away house hunting, but so far of no avail. You will of course
be of the first to be acquainted of such change; meantime dear I will
whenever possible give you the tidings of our transactions. All this has
been the outcome of endless negotiations, needless of detail, but in reality
nobody can really imagine. On the other hand should things go well, we
should reap the benefits of the past and near future with due recompense.*

*I was in Glasgow on business the weekend before last and spent Saturday
afternoon with Alick. He is liking the University well and looks well with
it too. The others are much as usual. My father is making little progress.
Trusting Kate dear you are well and happy.*

With fondest love, from your loving Peter.

Peter was delighted that Kate desired his company. They would have
had so much to talk about. In the last two years they had been very
busy; Kate establishing herself in New Zealand and Peter working for
BTH travelling around the country and going abroad. He had also
started a business to manufacture the seed sowing machine.

Peter would be anxious to know when Kate was going to come back.
They could then resume their relationship.

Due to the time delay in transporting letters to the other side of
the world, Peter was not yet aware that Jean would not work at St
Josephs. He was to find out in the next letter.

[? Late March 1914, the letter is undated.] *98, Claremont Road, Rugby*
My Dearest Kate,

In your letter of last week, you seemed dreadfully worried regarding Jean.
I read with interest all the passages of your letter and feel sure Kate dear,
the better course has been adopted by bringing Jean back beside you in
Napier. Poor girl, I do feel sorry for her, give her my best wishes and let
her treat it all as a misadventure, which we must join in expectations of
the best. One thing is obvious, she will do no good whatever by worrying
over it, this will only add to the already overloaded burden.

With reference to the gentleman you mention who is interested in Jean, I
should only be too pleased to communicate with him, such as you desire.
One thing of course remains open as you already know, my correspondence
at the present time is a very big item, and gets more so every day now .
However Kate dear that don't matter, anything at any time, tell him to
drop you a line and I shall be delighted to acknowledge same, especially
should it be on a question where I can be of any service whatever.

Bob has terminated with the Old Firm today and will be the receiver of
a grand testimonial tomorrow evening from the works, in recognition of
the good feeling which existed between himself and his fellowmen – this
is as you are no doubt aware, in the highest esteem.

I am remaining with the company. They could not see their way to release me, as I had been nominated for the position of Business Manager of the Foundry, Pattern shop and Purchasing Departments of all outside transactions relative to same. It is a big job, however worthy of a good trial.

We should be removing everything now to Lutterworth, when a suitable house can be had. Correspondence will of course be taken care of at the P.O.

We have had very rough weather lately today being cold, dull and uninteresting. This is where you Dear in the Colonies can smile over us and I trust you are well and happy.

With fondest love, from your loving Peter.

Why did Kate want Peter to correspond with Will? What exactly were the issues surrounding Jean and her speedy departure from Napier? Had she had an affair? Possibly the gentleman was a parent, a teacher or another member of staff? Or had she just flirted with and then rejected someone's advances? Could the girls' school still employ her?

Peter at the age of 25 would appear to be doing very well for himself. He and Bob had developed a mechanical seed sower which efficiently sowed fields. They had formed a business partnership with two other gentlemen and built factory premises in Lutterworth to mass produce the mechanical sower. Bob had been released from BTH to manage the production, but they would not release Peter and had given him a promotion. He intended to market his own development on his travels where and whenever he could.

April 21 1914. 98, Claremont Road Rugby.
My Dearest Kate,
It is nice, while in the mist of all our turmoil of business transactions to have your good wishes. I fully realise and know the extent, your interest

in our venture, reaches. We are just at the very worst point just now, with day and night making little difference, however I am pleased to say our efforts are bringing forth results of reasonable quality.

So far we haven't been able to fix a house at Lutterworth yet, but as the renting there is of a half yearly principle, we anticipate being able to satisfy our requirements by that time namely June.

One thing in nature is now in our favour long nights and very good weather that together with ambition keeps things moving very well. They are very anxious at 21 Grange Road to know how things are going, however I do not acquaint them with any more than is necessary, for it is not my wish to have much talk around home quarters before results are forthcoming.

So much for that lot Kate dear. I was pleased to hear from the passages of your long letter (thank you) that you have had a very interesting time of late, and I am looking forward to having the Photos you sent off. On horseback, my word, Kate you won't have much Gee Gee experience when you return to the old country. Never mind you enjoy yourself, you well deserve it and I am pleased indeed to hear, you have so many good friends in the colonies.

It is about time I stop Kate dear, as I have a lot to do before popping off. I am sorry to say My Father does not improve much and it will soon be 12 months since he got laid up. I was hoping the better weather might help him but apparently not.

Well Goodnight Kate dear, good luck and fondest love.

From your loving Peter.

In this letter Peter states *"when you return to the old country"* so it is possible that Kate was making plans and conveying this intention in her letters.

May 4, 1914 98, Claremont Road Rugby.
My Dearest Kate,

It is now three weeks since I had your letter saying the Photos had been forwarded. I do hope they haven't gone astray. Photos are so scarce nowadays aren't they Kate.

Reading over your last letter I was pleased to hear you had done so well since going to the Colony, also the financial side I think speaks well, also gratifying to know your labours have been rewarded in both directions namely financial and satisfaction.

Remember me to your pal Jean - tell her not to be downhearted, the sun will shine again and in a more positive direction, at least, we will hope so.

In four weeks' time I will be having 10 days holidays Dear, can I come to Napier? I am afraid no such luck - Lutterworth requires an enormous amount of attention. However Kate dear nothing is impossible. I may one day take a funny notion and have a trip your way. You will be saying if it only was true.

We are terribly busy just now Kate dear, our new works will be completed in about three weeks' time, and they do look well, of course only small, but small, in one sense, is large enough in another sense, until we can show in what direction progress can be made.

At home things remain much unchanged. Father does not improve, while the others are as usual. In all likelihood I won't have time to give them a visit this summer. Our Bowling Club opened a new Green on Saturday last, playing via the Rugby Council, quite a big affair. I do not intend following it much this season of course, the usual reasons.

I will now have to ring off. Hoping dear, you are happy and well.

With fondest love, from your loving Peter.

Why was Jean downhearted? I do not know. Unfortunately there was no information to answer this question.

Peter appears pleased that Kate has made many friends in New Zealand, and that she is satisfied in her job and receiving a good wage.

However his preoccupation with the construction of business premises gives him little time for anything else.

May 16. 1914 Pahiatua Box 101 Wellington. [A letter from Will].
My Dear Sister Kate,

Thanks awfully for your letter which I have just received, so sorry I haven't been able to answer before, I think perhaps one or two of my letters must have gone astray to Jean. I have sent one or two; I am not quite sure which from back-country places. Moutoa was one, but you can't depend on them, so in future I will only send from main places. You see Dear Sister a week seems to pass on these back-country places without seeming to have any time to do anything. For instance we were all day yesterday doing two places Ballance and Mako-Mako and never had anything to eat between 9 am and 10 pm. When we reached here, we had only had a cup of tea and a biscuit at Ballance. Then we had to put the car away and have supper which made it 11.15.

This morning we should have gone on to Weber and one or two other small places, but it is raining very heavy and roads are in a terrible state, so cannot start at present. Shall have to wait a little until it clears [See *Map 3*. It would appear that his sales territory was all of North Island. Places mentioned in the text are underlined].

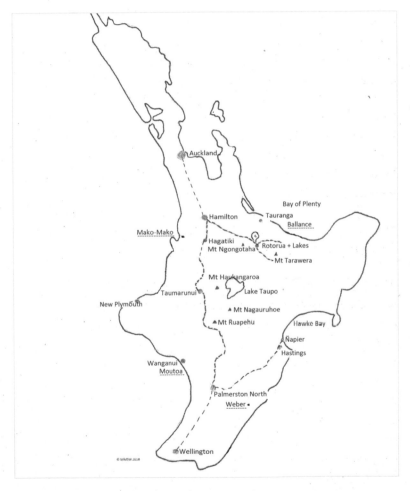

Will Berry's sales territory in North Island (Map 3)

No Dear Sister I am pleased to say not ill up to now, if I am so unlucky, I will manage to let you know some-way, rest assured that if you do not hear from me, it is because I am dodging about some very remote spots and not ill. If anything happens to me I will let you know at once, I promise you.

Well Dear Sister I can hardly describe how pleased I was to hear of Peter's success. It is something to recompense one for hard work, and a sure incentive for future perseverance; I must write and congratulate him on his good work and energy. If I address to BTH works Rugby will that find him? By the way Kate I still owe you some money which I have in hand for your box. I have almost forgotten how much, if you can let me know whether it is a Green Canvas Suit case 26" long you want or if it is a 26" long Cabin trunk, I can easily get it, and can send on.

Ernie is still at Nelson, and Miss Collett is over there, but what address I cannot say, will try and find out. Well dear sister must cease this time. Fondest love to Jean and very best Sisterly love to yourself.

Your loving brother Will.

Did Kate intend to return to Britain later in 1914 or early 1915, after spending two or three years abroad? The purchase of a large cabin trunk in May/June would suggest the possibility. The final term of the school year ended in December.

The next letter is from Peter. It is unaddressed.

June 1914.
My Dearest Kate,

I got your letter on Sunday morning after a long interval, you were saying I was long in writing and you wanted to pay me back, however Kate dear my correspondence was very much behind, much to my own dissatisfaction, but quite unavoidable, the wonder being now that I look back, how I have written so much.

You were talking of your holidays. I do hope you enjoyed them; no doubt you will be back in old style again.

Mrs D. I presume wrote you while I was away. I was having a good tour round the South of Belgium. I made the most of my time. From a business point of view it was a great success. Since then I have been to Scotland, having Saturday night and Sunday forenoon at home. I regret to say my Father is very ill indeed and I much doubt if he will ever be himself again. He told me none of them really knew how bad he was. I did feel sorry for him. He was saying he hadn't had a sleep for a fortnight. He cannot lie in his bed, cannot get outside and he is very weak and downhearted.

I don't know if I told you we had Jimmie down in Rugby for a week. It must have been very quiet for him and I only saw him twice. While going home he got into the wrong portion of the train and had from 2 am till 5 am to wait at Preston. However from accounts he was well enough pleased with his holiday, so that is all that matters.

I hope dear you are not having the heat too severe, for you were saying it was about the limit and likely to last much longer than we are accustomed to. Trusting you are happy and well,

With fondest love and best wishes from your loving Peter.

Little would Peter have known that events taking place hundreds of miles away in Bosnia would have a profound effect on his life. He was doing well - he had a good job with BTH and was a partner in a business venture which had almost completed premises in Lutterworth to manufacture seed sowing machines. He and Bob Duffus had developed this machine and held the patent. His job with BTH involved travelling around Britain and he would have been able to make contact with potential buyers once the manufacturing started. He had even been to the south of Belgium. Belgium had been host to a world trade fare the previous year; a celebration of industrial civilisation *(Ref 83)*. Quite ironic that this would be one of the first sites of battle within two months of his visit, and that he would later be involved in that theatre of war.

His father was seriously ill. He was suffering from heart failure. The heart no longer able to pump efficiently results in fluid building up in the lungs, abdomen and legs. The result is increasing shortness of breath which is worse on lying down, immobility, insomnia and general weakness. In 1914 treatment for heart failure would have been quite ineffectual. Modern potent drugs had not yet been developed. Peter was clearly struck by the deterioration in his father's health.

It is interesting that none of the letters from Mrs Duffus have survived. There are also very few letters from Kate's friends and relatives in Britain. Such letters would have helped to put more detail on the canvas but alas they are so few. Perhaps Kate just kept the letters that were special to her.

Alick started University in Glasgow in September 1913 and had completed his first year by June 1914.

The prelude to World War was already underway.

On 28 June 1914 the Archduke Franz Ferdinand was assassinated in

Sarajevo. A crisis developed in Serbia, and sadly this resulted in the so called civilised powers of Europe following the "domino effect" – if you attack us we will attack you. By the beginning of August; Austria, Hungary and Germany were at war with Russia and France. Britain joined France at midnight on 4 August because Germany refused to stop its invasion of Belgium *(Ref 7)*. The tragedy of World War One had begun. Peter would now lose his father just before the war started.

July 1914. 98, Claremont Road Rugby.
My Dearest Kate,

It seems ages since I wrote you last. Days have passed, weeks have past, but always the same; no time for writing.

They have been very trying times lately Kate dear, you will be sorry to hear Father has passed away and was buried on June 30th. No doubt it ended a very severe illness, which we all realise was only a matter of time, but oh how he suffered and how manly he endured it. We can only now hope he rests in peace.

My Mother has had strenuous hours ably assisted by John, James and Alick. In fact Alick was not aware of the seriousness of the case until he came home from the University. I am glad to say he got his Mathematics and German certificates, which is exceptionally good for the first year.

While I was home I had a long talk with Gilbert, your brother. He knew of course, how things were and said the last time he saw Father there was such a change. From his conversation all your people seem to be well.

The Business affair at Lutterworth has now started, having ended most of the preliminary efforts at any rate.

Having been run off my feet lately I am going off on Saturday morning for a motor tour in North Wales. This should be nice, in fact, very nice, provided the weather is with, and not against us. Ain't you coming Kate Dear? I will let you know how we go on. That is the next best thing I can do.

Glad to hear by your last letter that you had a good holiday, may they all be good ones, when they are holidays, so scarce and hard earned.

Hoping you are well and happy with fondest love,
from your loving Peter.

Peter would appear to have bought a car. Was he going to Wales with Bob, someone else, or perhaps a female companion? I do not know. He probably deserved his holiday now that his business enterprise was finally up and running.

His father's death certificate *(Ref 62)* states that James Taylor Wardlaw died from "Cardiac Dilatation and Nephritis". The date of death is 26 June 1914. He was only fifty one years old. It is likely that during his working life he was exposed to dust from glass and dangerous fumes from silica produced at high temperatures in the glass bottle making process resulting in silicosis of his lungs. This would have been the underlying pathology with heart failure the end result.

One hundred years ago there was little understanding or consideration of health and safety.

7

1914 AUGUST JOINING UP

August 1914. 98, Claremont Road Rugby.
My Dearest Kate,

It seems an age since I had a letter from you until last night; perhaps the War has upset everything. In fact I know it had in general business routine. I am pleased to hear you are well dear. A few passages of your letter did surprise me especially about John. First I have heard of course perhaps I am not in the know – what say you dear? However it may be possible even although I don't know.

Everything here is War mad and it is a question to know what will all happen within the next few days. Hundreds have left our works to join the colours and I am seriously thinking of having a word with Mother on the subject. Out of four sons at least one should represent the family. If I can join a Gunnery Battalion for the War period, I will do so, but it is the infantry they are in need of.

Business is absolute anyhow and on War Office or Admiralty work, it is break neck all the way. I see New Zealand is sending supplies and troops to the old country. Fancy the Russians are landing at Leith and then by train to Dover on route for France.

Mrs Duffus is on holiday for four weeks. Mother spent a week with her at Dunbar; that is where Mrs D's Aunt stays. From reports they had good weather and benefited by the change.

By the way I hear that Forbes (that is M Clark's "Boss") has had to close down owing to the War. Hard times ain't it dear.

Hoping you are as usual dear, happy and well.

With fondest love, your loving Peter.

I do not know exactly what issue Kate knew about John, that Peter did not, but it may have been to do with John's plan to marry his girlfriend Mary Morrison.

The war was on the way with young men joining up and factories changing to war production. Businesses that had thrived in peace time were closing down. British colonies were sending supplies and soldiers. Peter clearly felt a sense of duty as one of four sons to do his bit for the war effort. He would have to leave the BTH and the business in Lutterworth that he had only just set up. War production was taking over factories, and it is likely that his premises in Lutterworth would be converted for this purpose.

The reference to Russian soldiers arriving in Scotland on the way to France is interesting. This has been investigated by Dr David Clarke, an academic at Sheffield Hallam University *(Ref 8)*. In the opening weeks of the War, word spread that up to a million Russian soldiers had been shipped to Britain and were being transported through the country for action on the Western Front. Here the fighting was at a critical phase and such a large force of soldiers could influence the outcome.

The news even reached the ears of the Germans, apparently provoking them into strategic changes which allowed the Allies to stop them achieving a swift victory.

There was no truth in the reports; the massive force of Russians did not exist! Dr Clarke has traced the trigger for the rumour to events in August soon after war was declared, when railway movements around the country were subject to long hold ups. This allowed reservists to move from their barracks around the country to embarkation points on the south coast. These trains were hand signalled and moved at night with blinds drawn *(Ref 8)*.

One of the battalions involved was the Gaelic speaking 4th Seaforth Highlanders, whose bearded appearance and language appears to have given rise to many of the reports. In one Midlands station, a porter is said to have asked a group of Gaelic speaking soldiers where they were from – and to have misunderstood the reply "Ross Shire", as Russia *(Ref 8)*. Ross Shire is an area in the highlands of Scotland. Other Battalions may have sailed into the port of Leith rather than travel overland from the north of Scotland.

The next letter is from Will Berry letting Kate know what was happening with him since the War started.

21.8.1914 Box 101. Wellington.
My Dear Sister Kate,

Thanks ever so much for your letter, which was very cheering to read. So far things have not altered as regards myself, but I am expecting any minute to be called back to Wellington, and politely told that things are too bad to be kept on. A good many of the firms have already called their Travellers back, it certainly doesn't pay to keep one on the road.

The shopkeepers are very keen on not buying at present; they are making use of their present stocks. The scarcity of money is the greatest trouble. A good many firms demand cheques with order.

I have not yet received notice re the Navy, but according to the lists No 3 reserve are out, and it looks as if they mean to call up all the reserves.

Sorry you haven't heard from Mr Wardlaw lately, but he seems to have had some very bad luck with his father. Now the war has started, he will be worse off. I do hope his Father was much better by the time the War broke out.

Both my brothers have been called out, and all the relatives so we are doing our little bit alright. Ernie I hear is sick of Nelson and seems inclined to go to Frisco. Guess he had better wait a bit. Well love to Jean and yourself.

Your loving brother Will.

On the eve of World War One per-capita incomes in New Zealand were among the highest in the world; Ross & Glendining had benefited from this consumer confidence *(Ref 74)*. However the War had only just started and was already having a profound effect as Ross & Glendening laid off staff and others joined up.

Will was letting Kate know that he would soon be called up like the other Naval Reserves. His friend Ernie would wait to see what happen before making plans to sail for America.

August 30th 1914. 98 Claremont Road. Rugby.
My Darling Kate,

Excuse the paper [this letter is written on ledger lined account keeping paper] *but it is all I can lay my hands on for the time being. My mission in writing tonight is with reference to the European War. No doubt you will have read and read about it; and really it needs little explaining. The position is such that all young men between 19 and 30 have something serious to consider in their loyalty and duty to defend the Mother*

Country. I have been thinking seriously over the whole business for the past fortnight and in view of the fact that in our family 4 sons exist all within the age, I decided last night to volunteer for active service as a Gunner in the Royal Field Artillery. I leave Rugby on Tuesday about midday for Southampton for training purposes. The next step I will let you know of dear, having passed all the necessary physical and medical tests. The result is as fit as a fiddle. I daresay Kate dear that Mother will be worrying, but it is no good, it has to be faced and my own opinion is that all young men will have to go shortly, now dear let's hope that won't be necessary.

Need I say dear that I will write whenever possible, but we must be patient, rest assured I for one will do my utmost for the best. At the time of writing all the railways are closed for goods and passenger traffic to allow the troops, which have been brought from Canada and Russia, to be taken to Dover on route for France. It is simply awful just now Kate; only one good point is that so far the food supplies have been looked after. Address your letters as usual dear, they will be forwarded to me, but please don't be annoyed if thro' force of circumstances your letters seem few and far between.

Look after yourself Kate dear until we have the pleasure of each other's company again, I know you will Kate.

Trusting you are well and happy with all the love in the world to your dear self,

from your loving Peter.

A monumental decision for Peter but typical of all the young men who volunteered so soon after war was declared, perhaps they thought it would all be over quicker if they got involved. His background in engineering would make him well suited to gunnery. He was not tall, probably not much taller than Kate who is recorded as 5' 5" on her passport, so he may have felt unsuitable for the infantry.

There is no mention in this letter about the business venture which had dominated his life over the last eighteen months. Presumably their new premises and work force would be taken over by The War Office to further the war effort.

Soon after war was declared the BTH expanded its production to meet the demands of the Royal Navy. In company listings dating from 1914 but before the War started, BTH was described as "an electrical engineers and manufacturers of apparatus for electric traction, motors, alternators, switchgear, transformers and lighting. Specialities; "Curtis" turbines, horizontal and vertical types, "Mazda" metallic filament drawn wire lamps, railways, and tramway equipment. Employees 5600" *(Refs 3 & 67).*

How long would he have to wait for Kate now that war had started? His concern for her is evident as he mentions; *"Look after yourself Kate dear until we have the pleasure of each other's company again, I know you will Kate."*

8

1915 ARTILLERY TRAINING FOR ACTION

Peter had joined The Royal Field Artillery. This was part of The Royal Regiment of Artillery. It was made up of The Royal Horse Artillery which supported the Cavalry; The Royal Field Artillery with its horse drawn guns which supported the Infantry close to the front line, and The Royal Garrison Artillery with the massive destructive power of its heavy large calibre guns which were set back behind the front line *(Ref 60)*.

September 30th 1914 Chapletown Barracks Leeds. [The headquarters of the Cavalry and The Royal Horse Artillery].
My Darling Kate,

It seems ages since I wrote you dear, but I know full well how you will understand how things are here. I have only had one letter from you since I left Rugby, but I expect the boats are running anyhow, as I said before we must be patient. The country is in a very funny state. The future of events, there is no telling. Well Kate dear, when I first made up my mind to serve the colours, I addressed all the correspondence to John, asking him to talk and explain to mother. I wrote three times with no reply and it now appears Mother, John and Alick were on holiday and Jimmie was in digs, of course he never thought of calling at the house, with the result that Jimmie joined as well, during the week and nobody knew until the Saturday. You can imagine the turmoil, and John couldn't tell Mother for days after. She is very downhearted and although I have written to her, she has only pulled herself together last night, as I got a letter today.

Mrs Duffus promised to write to you. She has been very good Kate dear and has attended to my "needs" first class.

You will be pleased to hear I have got a stripe, having been promoted to Bombardier (PC8A). I had a nice letter from the Works, when they knew about it. That is the second I have had, I must say they have been exceptionally interested in my welfare. In fact the day I left, two of the managers marched in route from the Drill Hall to the station, one on each side, which showed how much they appreciated the occasion.

Bombardier Peter Wardlaw 1914
(PC8A)

Well dear the soldier's life is a very hard one, but I am glad to say it has agreed with me nicely and the hardness and strictness of it does not make any difference.

Being of course an Artillery Regiment, the Guns and Gun drill is first class, interesting at every turn. The first 2 weeks we were at Portsmouth and expected to go either to Woolwich, Aldershot or Salisbury Plain. Finally however we were drafted to Leeds, where we were billeted in a hotel living like Lords. As soon as I was promoted I had to come to Barracks. It is not as bad as I anticipated and of course don't mind roughing it. In fact I shouldn't like to think I couldn't be in the Army and not take the same care of myself as outside of it.

There has been great excitement the last three days as one of the Battery is leaving for the Front at 10 o'clock. Last night, what a scene, I thought Leeds were going mad, of course, really speaking, they only had the send-off they deserved - but what a row.

Our Battery have been attached to the 11TH Division of the 3rd Expeditionary Force, to be trained in readiness for January 13th 1915. The new Guns and Horses are expected this week. It is rumoured, on pretty good authority that the latter part of our training will take place in either Egypt or South Africa. Never mind Kate any of them will do for me. I should much like to go to South Africa, somehow I have a fancy to that country - I do not know why.

Sometime when I have an opportunity I will have my photo taken in uniform and send you one as soon as possible.

I had a letter from Mrs Duffus today saying they were flitting to Lutterworth having been fixed up with a suitable house. Sometimes I think Mrs Duffus having so much to do, will be taking too much out of herself. She will no doubt be better off at Lutterworth, being a rather nice country village.

Well dear, I will have to close now. A Barrack room is not too comfortable a place to write. Hoping you are well dear and with the best of wishes and fondest love,

from your loving Peter.

It would appear that Peter was fitting into army life rather well. In business he had proved himself to be ambitious, extremely capable, well organised and respected by his colleagues. It is not surprising therefore that the Army recognised his ability and promoted him within several weeks of him joining up. As the War progressed he would be promoted up the ranks.

It is interesting that at this stage he was able to write openly about the movements of his Brigade, where they were and where they were going, etc. Soon this would not be allowed as censorship would keep military activity even at home secret.

His recently widowed mother would be apprehensive with two of her sons joining up. Would she have to suffer more loss?

Wednesday 9/12/14 Leeds.
My Darling Kate,

I was beginning to think the ships bringing New Zealand correspondence, were amongst the many sunk by mines or German Warships, as I haven't heard from you for nearly six weeks or so. However dear they had only been delayed, for today I received no fewer than five.

For myself dear I haven't written nearly as often as I would have liked. The last time was while at Lutterworth on my way to the Gunnery school, where I remained for a month and glad to say I got on first class, so much so that on the third week I got another stripe, which promoted me to Corporal (PC8B & PC8C).

Corporal Peter Wardlaw
(PC8B)

Corporal Peter Wardlaw's gun crew with their 18 pounder
(PC8C)

The course was an exceptionally hard one and to make a success of it one had to devote every second of available time in studying. As you are no doubt aware dear the conditions in Barracks are not as good just now as in time of peace, and to make a success of things I hired a room in one of the big houses on the Sea Front where I went every evening, Saturdays and Sundays; all the time available, and a very funny thing happened. It now turns out that an Officer in the same regiment, with the same name as myself had stayed in that same house, while going through a nine month course in the same school.

Since coming home to Leeds I have been inoculated twice, meaning being confined to bed for 48 hours each time. This operation is supposed to be an excellent preventative against fevers common at the front.

I have got a lovely charger Kate dear. I think it used to be a hunter, before the Army took it over. So far both of us have been agreeing very well indeed, only of course my "legs" are no doubt sorer than the Gee-Gee's.

All being well I anticipate being home in Alloa during the New Year for about three days. Mother is expecting both Jimmie and I. It will be a change having two soldier ? boys at 21. If only Father had been alive what a difference it would have made, but never mind dear, we've got to face all these things, as you say dear. I would give all the world to have the pleasure of your company before going abroad, but I am afraid no such luck, for no doubt we'll be on the job shortly after New Year. In fact it is talked of being sometime in the middle of January.

I'll have to get changed for duty now, so Ta-ta until the next time. Hoping you're well and happy dear.

With fondest love, your loving Peter.

Why was Peter not writing much? The excuse that he was too busy studying at Gunnery School does not hold up to scrutiny. He states he had hired a room on the sea front at Whitby, and he was spending as much time as possible there. Could he not have found time to write when here away from the Gunnery School? Did he have another interest? Can you believe the story about the Officer with the same name?

The inoculation mentioned here was a vaccination against Typhoid fever caused by the bacterium Salmonella Typhimurium which can result in severe dysentery. This was definitely something to be prevented in the trenches.

There is mention here of the German Navy and the effects of the German U-boat campaign. Two days after war was declared, in retaliation for the Royal Navy's blockade of Germany, U-boats left their bases and started attacking Naval Vessels and supply ships to Britain. This activity intensified into 1915 with massive loss of ships and lives *(Ref 10)*.

[? Jan/Feb 1915. Undated letter.] *A Battery R.F.A... 58TH Brigade Chapletown Barracks. Leeds*
My Dearest Kate,

It's Sunday afternoon and for a change I have got a few minutes to myself. Would you believe it, nearly every post this week, I've had a letter from you, all written at the holidays. I'm so glad Kate dear you have an opportunity of a change, so as to see and enjoy the country in New Zealand. From your P.C.'s it must be nice indeed. The various places you have been could easily be visited for quite a good holiday, and I notice the Electricity is well equipped in many places.

I have just had a letter from home saying Mother has taken another house in Coningsby Place, the end opposite the Bowling Green and will take over same in May, so Kate dear no more 21 Grange Road.

You'll be pleased to hear I'm now Sergeant in our Battery (PC8D & PC8E) and of course the life, by having a Bunk to myself and dining in the Mess, is considerably changed. Plenty to do, to keep me out of mischief, and the little time goes like wild fire. I am enclosing two photos which I hope you will like, taken when I was a Corporal. The Officer in the group is an Edinburgh man and very decent indeed.

Mrs Duffus was saying Margaret has not been well. I expect it's the damp changeable weather we are having. For myself I'm just as usual doing as much as possible day by day and of course looking after myself.

Jimmy is still at Colchester, and as far as I can gather, he is doing well, although I must admit I should have written him long before now.

It's now bugle call for stable parade. Hay up. Bed down and water and feed, so I'll have to be off. By the way dear, I've been sent to take lessons in French, so I'll have less time than ever now. Glad to know you are still in Best of Health. With fondest love and the best of wishes,

your loving Peter.

Sergeant Peter Wardlaw (PC8D)

Sergeant Peter Wardlaw 1915 (PC8E)

Within six months of joining up Peter had been promoted to Battery Sergeant and was learning French. One would therefore think Higher Command was preparing his Brigade for the Front Line in France.

Peter comments about Kate writing to his widowed mother who had now moved out of the family home. He also appears surprised that places in New Zealand's country side are well equipped with electricity.

What military organisation had Peter joined?

An Artillery Brigade was the basic tactical unit of the field artillery of the British Army in the War of 1914-1918. It was made up of Brigade Headquarters and a number of gun batteries. At full establishment, a brigade of 18 pounder field-guns consisted of 795 men of whom 23 were officers *(Ref 25)*.

Brigade HQ was the management hub of the organisation and was staffed accordingly.

Batteries were usually lettered A to D. The first three A, B, and C were field gun units, and the fourth D battery consisted of a different weapon; the 4.5 inch howitzer. Each of the batteries usually had six guns and numbered 198 soldiers at full strength. Horses were used to move the guns.

The 18 pounder field-gun *(PC8C)* was the work horse of the Royal Field Artillery. It had a calibre of 3.3 inches and a range of 7,000 yards. It was capable of firing eight rounds per minute. It could therefore consume mountains of ammunition in a concentrated bombardment *(Ref 54a)*. A field- gun fired its shells on a low trajectory, often with the target in site. Shells were usually high explosive or shrapnel as required *(Ref 55)*.

The 4.5 inch howitzer lobbed its shell high into the air, so that it dropped more directly down on its target ie an enemy trench *(Ref 55)*.

Jimmie Wardlaw's Heavy Garrison Artillery Battery 1915
(PC8F)

Jimmie Wardlaw training with coastal defence guns
(PC8G)

The 58th Brigade remained attached to and supported the 11th Northern Division throughout the War. It was to see service in Gallipoli, Egypt and eventually France *(Ref 26)*.

The Heavy Artillery was a separate entity. They were known as the Royal Garrison Artillery and were equipped with much larger weapons than the Royal Field Artillery. Howitzers were from 6" to 9" bore, and there were also 60 pound heavy field guns. Such weapons required tractors rather than horses to move them, and some had to be deployed on rail tracks *(Ref 55)*.

Peter's brother Jimmie had joined the Heavy Artillery *(PC8F & PC8G)* and he would soon see action in France on the Western Front.

9

1915 GALLIPOLI - ANOTHER STALEMATE

By the spring of 1915 the earthworks of the Western Front stretched 1300 miles. Barbed wire, an invention of American cattle ranchers in the 1870's, was strung in belts between opposing trenches. The War was in stalemate so mobilisation to fight abroad did not happen for the 11th Division in January 1915, it had to wait.

The War Council had to come up with a plan to break the stalemate. They would attack the enemy in the "belly", by landing an army on the European shores of The Sea of Marmara or The Black sea, they could achieve a "third front" *(Map 4)*. However any force would have to get through the Dardanelles - the narrow waterway that connected The Aegean Sea with The Sea of Marmara. Unfortunately Turkey had closed the Dardanelles to shipping in November 1914. Russia had therefore declared war on Turkey and Britain's declaration followed *(Refs 13, 17, 21a & 28)*.

Initially it was the Navy alone, as proposed by Winston Churchill then First Lord of the Admiralty, that tried to force its way through the Dardanelles in February and March 1915 by bombarding the Turkish Forts that defended the route. Unfortunately this was unsuccessful and, with German help, the Turks reinforced their position.

In March 1915 General Sir Ian Hamilton, aged 62, a veteran of many conflicts including the Boer War, was put in charge of the expedition that became known as The Gallipoli Campaign. At this time there was already a substantial force of New Zealand and Australian soldiers in Egypt. They had been mobilised for action on the Western Front, but

Gallipoli - The Third Front (Map 4)

together with reinforcements from Britain and France along with the Navy, they would make up the Battle Group in the Dardanelles. The conflict to establish a "third front" began on 25 April 1915. This day became ANZAC Day and commemorates what was about to unfold.

The New Zealanders and Australians were landed before dawn at what is now known as "Anzac Cove" and by the afternoon were fighting for their survival, facing steep ridges and gullies, the most difficult terrain on the peninsula. The Anzac troops faced determined Turkish defenders and could barely hold their bridgehead. At Cape Helles, the main objective, there was fierce fighting and heavy casualties.

Troops across the peninsula experienced dysfunctional command, poor artillery support, severe heat, little food, dehydration and high casualties. Putrefying human flesh in the heat would have attracted swarms of flies as dysentery and diarrhoea spread among the soldiers; horrific. It was another stalemate. At Anzac there was a truce on 24 May to bury the dead littering no-man's land *(Refs 7,12,13,14,15,17,21a,28,47,54 & 57)*.

Reinforcements would be needed if any progress was to be made in Gallipoli. It would be to this theatre of conflict that Peter's Brigade would be sent.

Peter was still in Britain at this time. He was not yet aware where his Brigade would be deployed.

[? April or May 1915. Undated letter.] *Milford Camp. Surrey.*
My Darling Kate,

By the above you'll see we've shifted from Leeds, but whatever has become of your letters. I haven't had any for; I believe a month, although the last bunch consisted of nearly eight. Perhaps mine are somewhat similar. I hope they are running fairly regular, but we have no control over these things and I don't see the papers so much now to find out how the mails are running.

At present I can't say dear how long it will be before we go off. Somehow or other I don't think it will be long now, but they don't furnish us with much information on these points.

I had a letter from home this week. Mother has got settled down in 15 Coningsby Place, thanks to the assistance of Alick, while on holiday. He seemed to enjoy the flitting immensely. John's marriage I understand is now fixed for the middle of June. I don't know dear if I'll be able to attend or not, as I said before perhaps I'll be far enough away ere then.

James is being shifted from Colchester to Salisbury Plain, shortly, so I expect he too will be getting forward. Now I had news through Mother that he had been kicked by a horse and it is questionable if it won't leave a bad scar on "His Complexion". I haven't been able to see him since he joined, but I expect Kate dear that the roughing may be testing his patience etc.

I'm sending under separate cover a photo I had taken just before leaving Leeds. I sent a few to Scotland and they all seem delighted with it. I hope you'll like it dear. To see me now, I'm afraid you would know a change. I'm as black as can be, the skin on my face is simply burned away and doesn't it give me "what for" during the heat of the sun.

There is talk of a few hours leave before we go. Should this be so, and I've got time to go north to Alloa, I'll endeavour to see Gilbert on my travels.

I expect you're feeling the turmoil of the times, more and more every day where you are dear; if this affair lasts much longer I am afraid there will be no men left at the finish. Still we can't govern these things. Let me know as regular as you can dear how you're getting on. I expect you are writing every week, but they're not coming through. I may get another bunch altogether any day. I'll write as often as I can, but the facilities etc., are practically nil now.

Remember me to Jean, tell her I hope to see her again "Someday".

With fondest love and Kindest Regards, Your loving Peter

Witley Camp was a temporary army camp on Witley Common, Milford, Surrey, England *(Ref 9)*. The camp had been set up in the early stages of the War probably by the Canadian Army. Witley was considered an ideal situation for training artillery. It was surrounded by a large area of reasonably flat land covered with gorse and heather, which gave opportunities for a variety of manoeuvres. The sandy soil could readily be moved to construct gun pits, conceal weapons and improve camouflage.

Peter hoped to meet up with Kate's brother Gilbert and later share the gossip with Kate. Family ties were growing stronger. He also hoped to see Jean someday.

[? May 1915. Undated letter.] *Witley Camp. Surrey.*
My Darling Kate,
The days keep slipping in and we are still at the above. I expect however within the next few days to be off, but just you keep addressing to Lutterworth. They will send everything forward to me. How are you getting along Kate dear? It seems such a time since I heard from you, but I expect someday soon to receive about half a dozen, such as usually occurs.

I seem to have but little news this week. I hope you had the photos alright. I'm enclosing the Royal Artillery Motto, which is really a miniature Cap Badge in the shape of a Broach (PC9A), its only Brass of course, but should you be particularly keen on the design I daresay dear you could have it dipped.

I'm not sure if I told you last week that Alick had passed in all his subjects

Cap Badge Royal Artillery Motto UBIQUE QUO FAS ET GLORIA DUCUNT 'Everywhere where right and glory lead' (PC9A)

this year and is now endeavouring to take his degree with Honours namely his B.S.C.

Have you heard about Alick Dawson of Hallpark Sauchie, (I believe he is a distant relative of yours) he was killed in a smash on a motor cycle. Hard times isn't it? You remember him being at the Grange the day you were there? How time changes things; - just fancy then and today.

Now it's about time I concluded this scribble dear, only I thought a line in whatever a condition would be better than none, only there is such a lot to be done Kate.

I'll put an extra stamp on dear for fear it just exceeds the weight.

Well Good night dear and all the luck in the world to you.
With Kindest Regards,

Your loving Peter.

31 May 1915. [Dated from information contained within the letter.]
Reg. No. 10626. A Battery 58th Brigade, R.F.A. Camp. Milford Surrey.
My Darling Kate,

Never mind the address. I must put it on, its force of habit dear. I've just received two nice letters from you Kate together with a snap shot. My word you must be getting on with your riding exercises, when you can go out bareback, you have my sympathy dear. I know what it is, not to be able to stand up, sit down or lay in bed. The photos were alright Kate as you remarked dear you do look happy and keep on looking happy, that's the game. I'm glad you liked mine.

Now Kate before I start working my way through the home news, excuse me bringing up anything I wrote in my last letter dear, because really I don't know where my last conversation with you terminated. In the first place as far as I can gather a gloom has been cast over the old place, due to so many of the local Territorials being killed at the front.

Did you know George Grant? Who went about with John? He is a Glasgow chap I believe and was very intimate with Nellie Morrison [Peter's older brother John was engaged to Mary Morrison, Nellie's sister]. *Well to make a long story short, John is being married a fortnight today (namely 14/6/15) while news has reached Alloa that George has died of wounds at the front.*

They are all terribly anxious about me being at the marriage but, I am told tonight to take this weekend for farewell leave as we go out sometime before 14th June. So will be busy soon dear. Our Division was inspected by the King today. Quite an extraordinary sight I assure you.

I haven't heard much of Jimmy, but should have "All the latest" when I reach home. Progress seems to be the word to use with reference to affairs at Lutterworth.

I'm up to my eyes with parades so will get this posted for the mail. I will write you from home on Sunday. So look out for Alloa Gossip next time. With all good wishes and Kind Regards,

From your loving Peter.

What a difference from the summer of 1912 when Peter had been surprised by his brother John and the Grant brothers when they took him to the Morrison's *"neat little garden party at Dirliton Gardens"*. What sorrow for John's future sister-in-law Nellie; her man was dead. George may have been John's best friend. This would have cast a gloom over the wedding which should have been a happy time.

The *"local Territorials"* refers to The Argyll and Sutherland Highlanders Regiment; famous as the Thin Red Line at the Battle of Balaclava in the Crimea, 1854. As the War progressed six soldiers in this regiment would be awarded the Victoria Cross *(Ref 73)*. Brave men.

[? 6/6/15 Undated letter.] *Witley Camp. Milford. Surrey.*
My Darling Kate,

It's been a lovely summer Sunday and I've been out on my horse for a nice exercise. It brought to mind my thoughts regarding your experience in that line. How are you fairing Kate dear, had a fall yet? I'm sure you'll be quite an expert on your return (PC9B & C).

I received the other day a message of yours via Mrs Duffus with reference to your wanting to get something for James and myself. It is far too good of you Kate and I'm sure I speak for both of us in acknowledging your kindness. For myself I got a nice little watch for seeing in the dark - exceptionally good for our night movements, which means so much to us.

We are now having our weekend of farewell leave. I am leaving mine until the last, so as if possible to be at John's wedding which takes place on June 14th. But I am afraid I will be away before then.

Isn't the War getting dreadful, my word, there's no saying how far it will go yet. I hear there are many casualties affecting people in Alloa and quite a gloom over many homes.

How are the letters running dear? Do you have many? Or what? I see it's scarcely safe for a boat to be almost anywhere now. Fancy the Lusitania being sunk. It's too sad to think of all that innocent suffering isn't it? Kate.

Don't be downhearted dear if you don't receive much news, rest assured I'll write whenever I have a chance, but it is so difficult.

I note with much pleasure your remark regarding how you have looked after what you have so hard earned since going to the Colony. I congratulate you Kate dear and I sincerely trust the rest of your time in the Colony, before returning to the Old Country, will be as prosperous.

I'll have to stop now dear, with all my love, and the best of wishes,

Your loving Peter.

Kate and Jean horse riding in New Zealand (PC9B)

There are no letters sent from Alloa, however Peter did get to his brother's wedding to Mary Smith Morrison. The marriage record in Alloa dated 15 June 1915 has Peter's signature as a witness to the wedding.

I do not know if Peter met up with Gilbert or not, but he had conveyed his intention to Kate.

The consequences of war were taking their toll. Soon Peter would experience the carnage first hand. It would appear from this letter that

Battery Sergeant Peter Wardlaw with his charger (PC9C)

Kate wanted to return to "the Old Country". However the sinking of the Lusitania, a passenger liner, with the death of 1198 passengers, and U-boats apparently everywhere, would have made her reconsider her intentions. Again she would delay her trip back to the UK.

10

NAVAL ACTION

By early 1915 all nations had lost the illusion that the War could be won quickly and took measures to gain an advantage. Britain had established a naval blockade of German ports from the onset of the War. Germany had responded with a U-boat campaign which had intensified to "unrestricted submarine warfare" by January 1915 *(Ref 10)*.

The Cunard liner Lusitania was an impressive luxury liner with 30,000 tons displacement, and a top speed of 26 knots. She had twice won the Blue Riband for the fastest Atlantic crossing but lost it permanently in 1909 to her sister ship the Mauretania *(Ref 82)*.

She had elegant passenger accommodation and safety features: a double bottom and watertight compartments to prevent a Titanic type disaster. Though the British Admiralty did not requisition the ship, it did require that some of the hold space be reserved for the transport of war materials from America *(Ref 10)*.

On 1 May 1915 the Lusitania left New York with 1257 passengers, 197 of them Americans. There were also various items in the hold including 4200 cases of rifle cartridges, 1248 cases of infantry shells, and 18 cases of fuses. Clearly this information was never common knowledge in Britain, but information in New York papers on 1 May 1915 warning that the Lusitania was "liable to destruction" in the war zone, would suggest that the Germans were aware of her cargo *(Ref 10)*.

The Lusitania was struck by the German U-boat "U-20" on Friday 7 May 1915 off the coast of Ireland as it headed for the Port of Queenstown. The U-boat Captain Walter Schwieger fired just one torpedo which blew a hole in the side of the ship. There was a large second explosion, thought to be from munitions carried on board. The ship sank in just eighteen minutes *(Ref 10)*. In Germany a medal was issued to commemorate the achievement. In Britain a darkly sarcastic medal was issued to indicate a war crime had been committed *(PC10A & PC10B)*.

Box with the Lusitania Medal. The sinking of The Lusitania caused outrage and revulsion in Britain. To commemorate the atrocity a medal was issued. The dark sarcasm is poignant. This was a war crime.
(PC10A)

A
German Naval Victory

"With joyful pride we contemplate this latest deed of our navy."
Kölnische Volkszeitung, 10th May, 1915.

This medal has been struck in Germany with the object of keeping alive in German hearts the recollection of the glorious achievement of the German Navy in deliberately destroying an unarmed passenger ship, together with 1,198 non-combatants, men, women and children.

On the obverse, under the legend "No contraband" (*Keine Bannware*), there is a representation of the *Lusitania* sinking. The designer has put in guns and aeroplanes, which (as was certified by United States Government officials after inspection) the *Lusitania* did *not* carry, but has conveniently omitted to put in the women and children, which the world knows she *did* carry.

On the reverse, under the legend "Business above all" (*Geschäft über alles*), the figure of Death sits at the booking office of the Cunard Line and gives out tickets to passengers, who refuse to attend to the warning against submarines given by a German. This picture seeks apparently to propound the theory that if a murderer warns his victim of his intention, the guilt of the crime will rest with the victim, not with the murderer.

Leaflet present with the medal (PC10B)

There was a massive outcry in both Britain and America, but America would not be dragged into the conflict. However in August after further sinking of passenger liners and American deaths the German

Kaiser advised U-boats not to attack passenger vessels *(Ref 10)*. Obviously there would be grey areas.

U-boats were rather an unknown entity at the beginning of the War. Germany had invested heavily in them and that investment had brought results. Thousands of tons of shipping carrying goods to and from Britain were destroyed in the first six months of the War. Although Britain had developed the underwater bomb which was detonated by water pressure, the "depth charge" *(Ref 71)*, without the means to locate a submarine when underwater the U-boat was almost invincible *(Ref 10)*. It would be a long time before underwater acoustics could identify U-boats.

As shipping losses mounted The Royal Navy devised the "decoy ship", a merchant vessel with concealed weapons to lure the U-boat into close range where it could be attacked and destroyed.

One of the first successes was achieved by my name sake, possibly a distant relative, in July 1915. In the sea off the north coast of Scotland U-boats were destroying colliers taking coal to the naval base at Scapa Flow to fuel the warships. One collier named Prince Charles had been fitted with concealed guns. The crew was both Naval and civilian *(Ref 10)*.

On the evening of 24 July 1915, the Prince Charles encountered the Danish steamer Louise, which had been halted by the U-boat "U-36". This U-boat spotted the Prince Charles and opened fire on the collier with her deck gun at long range. Royal Navy Lieutenant Mark Wardlaw, in command of the Prince Charles, halted the collier and ordered the civilian crew to abandon ship in an apparent panic. The "U-36" then closed in to finish off the Prince Charles *(Ref 10)*.

Lieutenant Wardlaw decided to lure the submarine in as close as possible then he blew a whistle. Wardlaw's gun crews dropped the screens that hid the two guns and immediately opened fire on the "U-36". The Germans were startled, climbed back into the submarine in a hurry and tried to dive, but the shots from the Prince Charles struck the U-boat. As her crew abandoned ship, she went down. The Prince Charles rescued fifteen of the thirty three German crewmen *(Ref 10)*.

This episode showed that decoy ships could work. The secret was kept during the War and these special service ships became known as "Q-ships". Later in the War Alick, Peter's youngest brother, would join the Royal Naval Reserve on the Clyde and would see active service on a "Q-ship".

11

1915 GALLIPOLI NEW ARMY TO BREAK DEADLOCK

The next letter from Peter is just a fragment but tells Kate that he was off to war.

1 July 1915. Devonport.
My Darling Kate,

We are now embarking at Devonport on the Knight Templar with an escort of 22 Destroyers. It is awful warm dear and such a lot to be done; I had your letter on the 29th along with the photos which are splendid indeed Kate…. Drop me a line and I…….

This is all that remains of this letter. We, I believe refers to the Royal Field Artillery, probably just the 58th Brigade with its horses. The 11th Division Infantry sailed from Liverpool *(Ref 16)*.

Map 5 of Europe and the Mediterranean gives some information regarding the movement and deployment of Peter's 58th Field Artillery Brigade, part of 11th Division between July 1915 and July 1916.

The Knight Templar *(PC11A)* was a commissioned escort ship which had been used to transport troops from New Zealand to Egypt earlier in 1915 *(Ref 59)*. It was well suited to the needs of the Royal Field Artillery because large areas on board had been converted to stables for horses *(Ref 58 & PC11B)*. Information later on would suggest that equipment such as the field guns were transported in a different ship.

According to information from Second Lieutenant Bob Brag who was in command of 'A' Battery RFA 58th Brigade, they passed Malta in the Mediterranean arriving in Egypt where they stayed in Alexandria for two weeks before leaving in late July; they reached the Island of Lemnos on 1 August 1915.

Peter sailed from Devonport to the Mediterranean 1 July 1915 with 'A' Battery 58th Brigade RFA 11th Division British Mediterranean Expeditionary Force in the Knight Templar accompanied by 22 Destroyers. They passed Malta on the way to Alexandria Egypt.

From Alexandria they sailed in late July to the island of Lemnos 1 August for the Suvla landing in Gallipoli.

Departed Gallipoli 19 December 1915 to the island of Imbros. Sailed to Alexandria arriving January 1916 in position to defend the Suez Canal 19 February 1916.

Sailed from Egypt on 3 July 1916 to Marseille France in the Front line on The Somme 27 July 1916 (Refs 12 and 30).
(Map 5)

The escort ship, Knights Templar Peter sailed to Egypt on this ship from Devonport on 1 July 1915 (PC11A)

The Knights Templar with areas converted to stables to transport horses (PC11B)

Fortunately I came across information from Bob's war diary contained in a book dedicated to the lives of the Brag family and their contribution to crystallography and science. I am most grateful to the author John Jenkin for collating this information. This provides factual information about Peter's first encounter with the enemy which he could never have recorded in his letters to Kate.

Lieutenant Bob Brag was in charge of four guns in 'A' Battery, and Peter was the sergeant attached to that Battery; they would have been well acquainted. They were part of three divisions of the New Army that were to make a major attempt to break the deadlock at Gallipoli in the "August Offensive" *(Refs 7,12,13,14,15,16,17,21a,28,29, 34 & 48)*. As the Sergeant of 'A' Battery, Peter would have been involved in the events that followed.

The intention was to drive inland behind the Turkish position at Anzac, and capture the high ground cutting the Turkish communications. Unfortunately the landing turned into a fiasco.

The 11th Division started moving ashore at Suvla on 6 August, but the 58th Artillery Brigade was not among them. Landing took place in stages, the Artillery last. 'A' Battery of the 58th Brigade waited three days before going ashore but was forced to camp for several days until the rest of the Brigade arrived. Their guns were landed further south at Anzac Cove and were eventually brought up the coastal track by horses.

A week after landing (15 August) the Brigade was in position near Charak Cheshme and Hill 10 *(Map 6)*. Here they supported an infantry attack to gain high ground on the Tekke Tepe ridge; 'A' Battery fired on Turkish trenches and distant targets. Unfortunately the attack was not a success.

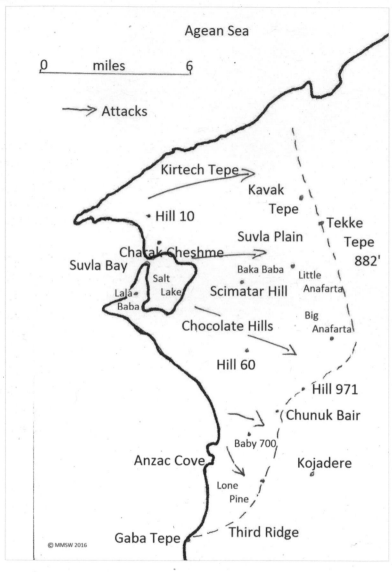

The Suvla landing
(Map 6)

On 21 August the 11th infantry division attacked high ground to the South of the Suvla Plain. Unfortunately for the infantry, the Turks had strengthened their position over the previous two weeks since the landing *(Map 6)*. 'A' battery took up position in the valley below the Tekke Tepe ridge and Baka Baba to support the infantry. Again this attack failed due to heavy counter fire from Turkish positions. There were many casualties.

'A' Battery was about to experience a greater loss with the death of their commanding officer. On 1 September sitting in the trenches with another officer censoring letters, an unexploded shell came through sand-bags and severed Lieutenant Brag's leg; he was taken to the Hospital Ship Nevasa in Suvla Bay, but died on board *(Ref 12)*.

This would have been Peter's first experience of battle and it may have been Peter's first experience of death among his comrades in 'A' Battery. He had lost his commanding officer, perhaps a friend. The reality in the vagaries of war is that it could have been him. As he was the Sergeant of 'A' Battery would more be expected of him now?

Inexperience and poor leadership had failed to take the initiative. Any initial advantage was lost as the Turks, led by the dynamic Mustafa Kemal, (later President Ataturk of Turkey) and helped by the Germans, constantly improved their position on the high ground. Some had watched British troops sunbathing on the beach below.

Commander in Chief, General Hamilton's Third Despatch describes in detail how the Gallipoli Campaign progressed and sadly failed. He is critical of General Stopford for his failure to lead the New Army Divisions appropriately and seize advantage when presented, in particular the lack of momentum that prevailed.

Peter's 58th Brigade is mentioned in General Hamilton's Despatches, taking part in the Battle to gain possession of the ridge - Kiretch Tepe Sirt. General Hamilton is complimentary of the Royal Artillery; "By their constant vigilance, by their quick grasp of the key to every emergency, by their thundering good shooting, by hundreds of deeds of daring, they have earned the unstinted admiration of all their comrade services. Where all fought so remarkably the junior officers deserve a little niche of their own in the Dardanelles record of fame. Their audacity in reconnaissance, their insouciance under the hottest of fire, stand as fine example not only to the Army, but to the nation at large" *(Ref 28)*. Compliment indeed.

The first letter from Peter to Kate is after the initial action had settled down. The small territorial hold that the Allies had achieved in the Dardanelles had now reached a stalemate, just like the other fronts, entrenchment prevailed. So much sacrifice for so little gain.

August 31/1915. Somewhere on the "Peninsula ".
My Dearest Kate,

Well, well and how are you dear? The letters do take a time to get here. First to England, then back again to here. Just fancy two or three days ago I had yours of May 17th, I believe it was, however I expect mine will go direct from here to New Zealand.

Glad to say I am keeping well and above all it is not nearly as warm as in Egypt. I've had quite a few letters from home this week. Alick is on a boat for the August month just to keep himself out of mischief, till the University reopens. Jimmie has gone to France and I expect to hear from him any time now.

With John being out of the house Mother is naturally all alone, and I imagine she is worrying slightly, however these things have to be so haven't they dear. Things are exceptionally busy in Lutterworth. The BTH practically keeps them going day and night and Bob has his load very full indeed. However that is what is wanted and I think the new venture should surely have found a good footing by now. [This would indicate that his business in Lutterworth was helping the BTH with war production].

Mrs Duffus and family have gone to Scotland for the usual summer trip. A month I believe this time, after calling at both their houses. Alloa is to be visited on the way back, and I am expecting any day to hear the progress of their "Tour". Annie will no doubt keep up her reputation, while Margaret must be having the cold, etc. and sore teeth poor girl. She does suffer.

By the way Kate I had a small souvenir scarf, of one of the places en route, sent on to you directly. You received it dear? Then the day we started for here, I had a flashlight card sent out. Did this arrive at its destination? Let me know, will you? When next you write.

I expect you'll be having your "winter holidays" just now and I do hope you have a good time dear. But I expect the colonies are now more or less like the old homeland, more or less all war and the resulting properties of same.

I'll have to stop now dear. Will write again at next opportunity. Trusting you are well and happy.

With fondest love, your loving Peter.

PS. Did you get the PC's? I find only a few reached home.

The tone of this letter is rather wistful. Perhaps he was missing the "nice things" in life that others at home took for granted. Perhaps he was lonely and yearned for the impossible; Kate's company.

Because letters were censored Peter had to be careful how he conveyed information. He was not able to say anything directly about his war experience. He mentions that Jimmie is in France. The fact that he is at the Front is inferred. The boat that Alick is on in his summer holidays may well be him training as a Royal Naval Reservist. It is not surprising that his mother was *"worrying slightly"* with three of her sons now in service.

His factory premises in Lutterworth were busy. He does not state what they were manufacturing but it would be to help BTH with the war effort.

Life for these young children in the holidays would appear to continue as normal, but the War was taking its toll at home and his last remark is poignant, knowing what a hammering the New Zealand Army took in Gallipoli. Kate would be well aware of the Colonies' contribution to the War effort through newspaper articles, returning casualties and shared grief with those who suffered loss.

Sept 26. 1915. [This letter has no address but his Brigade was still on "The Peninsula".]

My Dearest Kate,
This letter must necessarily be very short, only as I want to catch the Mail. Well Kate dear you talk about letters; within the past 8 days I've had I should think 9 from you. They came three at a time. I'm glad you liked the photos. When I sent one home, Mother had to send to Leeds for a dozen or so to give out to so and so, etc. Of course I didn't trouble with all these small affairs. One thing I must give due credit to Mrs Duffus for

forwarding on your letters. No sooner are they at Lutterworth than they are re-posted for here.

I'm enclosing some "Flags", some of which are rather nice, others rather "Dirty" (perhaps they'll clean). However they've all been collected from Cigarettes issued to the "Tommies" in the trenches. Personally I don't smoke my share, but exchange them for the "Flags".
About all the news from home is that Mother and Alick have been to Dunbar for a week.

Hoping you are well and happy,

With fondest love, your loving Peter.

I remember as a boy that there was a metal biscuit tin which contained flags from cigarette packets. I now know their history. However these must have been lost when the family house was cleared.

9/10/15. [Unaddressed letter]
My Dearest Kate

I had two letters of yours with the last mail (Wednesday) just fancy; to show you how erratic the system goes. One letter June 11th, the other July 17th, but never mind dear, when I get a mail it's usually about 3 or 6 from you all in a heap, that's when the ship doesn't go down.

Mrs Duffus has returned from her usual holiday in the north, unfortunately it has been somewhat spoiled due to the children not being well. Alloa was visited for one night only; however Mother was pleased to have Mrs Duffus although only for that period.

Alick and Mother have been to Dunbar for a week, staying with Mrs

D's Aunt who keeps the Castle Hotel there. They both seemed to enjoy the change. Alick by now will be back in Glasgow for the Winter Term. I think I told you he was going in for taking his degree with honours. Jimmy is still in France, but up to the time of writing he hasn't written me, and I expect he is like myself minus the writing feeling very often.

By your letters dear you seemed to be very shorthanded and busy. You have my sympathy and I trust all is well long before now.

I was much interested to hear about the wounded from the Dardanelles. It sounds much like home to read of accounts such as these.

I'm enclosing a few more Flags I obtained here. The N. Z. Flag is included. They seem rather nice.

In one of your letters you said something about sending a Photo (a group), but although I've received about 8 letters since, no Photo has been enclosed. Has the letter (gone west) or the Camera (failed to do its duty)? Of course some time previous to that I had 2 Photos. One of Yourself and one taken with Jean. I sent quite a few before leaving Whitley. Did you receive them? I'll have to stop now dear. Trusting you are well and happy,

with fondest love Peter.

The tragedy of the Gallipoli campaign had touched Kate in Napier as she described to Peter her experience of seeing wounded men return to New Zealand. He could commiserate with her but put nothing of his own experience in writing.

The small green envelope which contained this letter states "On Active Service. Note – Correspondence in this envelope need not be censored regimentally. The contents are liable to examination at the

Base. The Certificate on the flap must be signed by the writer. I testify on my honour that the contents of this envelope confer nothing but private and family matters". It is duly signed *"P.H. Wardlaw"*.

There is quite a contrast in the nature of the paper making up the letters written from the trenches. It is thinner and after a hundred years the ink has faded to a greater degree than in Peter's letters written in Britain. It would seem that Kate wrote far more letters to Peter than he did to her, but he was limited in both available time to write when on active service and the limited content he could mention. There were obvious issues with the mail, some letters did not arrive for months, some not at all and others all at once. These letters would have had a good psychological effect on Peter. He was also keen that photographs should be exchanged.

The next letter in chronological order is from Kate's sister-in-law, Nellie, Gilbert's wife.

4th Nov. 1915. 21 Queen Street. Alloa.
My Dear Kate,

As you say in last week's letter that I'll be wondering why you have been long in writing, so you will be saying about me. I asked Rena [the younger of Kate's two sisters. She is mentioned later as Aunty] *to post your paper for the last week and to write you a short note for me, which I hope she did. She would tell you how busy I am meantime. I seem never to be off my feet night or day.*

It is now three weeks tomorrow since Daddy [her husband, Kate's brother Gilbert] *came home from the hospital and is quite an invalid still and confined to bed. He gets up sometimes but often feels worse after it owing to the very weak state he is in. If he was free of pain I think he would get on alright but he suffers terribly at times - with nerve pains and flatulence and some nights we get no sleep at all.*

One night last week he took very ill and I had to get up, dress and call for a neighbour and then we got Aunty who stayed all night and since then she has come along every night about nine and leaves again after breakfast. It was Gil's own suggestion as he thought I should not be alone especially at night. Meantime Aunty has no engagement up till New Year so it is lucky for me.

I manage the nursing alright, but it is a comfort just to know there is someone in the house. I am only trusting that I will get strength to continue as I am doing, but it is very hard especially as any improvement is so slow.

Nan was ill for ten days with a nasty chill, but is better again. You guess I could have done nicely without her being ill, but misfortunes never come singly. We have many visitors too and it all means work answering the door.

Isn't this a dreadful time we are living in? So depressing in every way, and when there is trouble at home it seems awful. Some days I am in the dumps, other days I am quite bright and able to look on the bright side. We must all wait with patience until we see how things will turn out.

They have started going from door to door canvassing for recruits now so it is very serious. Soon there will be no men left. Glad to know your boy [Peter] is still safe. Cheer up there's trouble everywhere. Much love from all.

Always yours Nellie.

Poor woman she was finding it hard to cope. Her husband was

dying. He had up to recently been well. His symptoms had resulted in abdominal surgery. He had not made the expected recovery. He had complications and was in constant pain. He could not move and was getting weaker by the day. The most likely event here was that of acute appendicitis complicated by generalised peritonitis. The latter was almost certainly fatal in the pre-antibiotic era.

Kate would have found the news of her brother's deterioration in health distressing. She would also be worried about Nellie and her nieces Lalla and Nan. She would have liked to help, however the harsh reality of her situation was only too apparent; she was on the other side of the world. Would this have made her more determined to get back to Britain?

The next letter from Peter has no address.

7th Nov 1915
My Dearest Kate,

It's Sunday again, my "Old" writing day. But writing Kate dear under the circ's is a very funny problem at times. But Kate I must give you the verdict for writing. Why, when we do have a mail it's customary to have about three or four from you.

There seems to be little to write about. Jimmy is still in France. Alick at the University. John, I presume, busy with his new venture and last but not least Mother alone at 15 C. Place, doing away in her own way. I haven't had a letter from Lutterworth for over a fortnight, however I think things are going well there. I was sorry indeed Kate to read about you having cut your hand so badly. That's the worst of those sharp knives. I sincerely hope dear to have better news in your next letter.

But never mind Kate I should like to see you persevere with your carving. As you know however the tools must be sharp, the only remedy is as given out in the first stages of wood working. The hand not actually holding the Tool must be in rear of same. How's that fancy me going way back to the early days of my apprenticeship.

But Kate I really must stop. I'm enclosing a few more "Flags" I got here. Trusting you're in good health and spirits dear.

With Fondest love, your loving Peter.

Kate had taken to wood carving as a hobby. She would have seen how readily the Maoris took to carving on her travels. What a contrast to Peter's life of war. They were experiencing such different things as the war raged on but Peter could not tell her due to censorship of letters from a war zone.

Sadly cutting her hand, Kate would have had difficulties doing her job possibly for several weeks depending how bad the cut was and which hand was involved.

Nov. 13th 1915. [Unaddressed letter]

My Dearest Kate,

I've had three letters from you this week. That's how I usually get them, you know, about three or four at a time. However dear I was pleased to hear that your Influenza cold has left you, but poor Jean seems to have rid you of it.

Sorry to hear that Gilbert had to undergo an operation. I sincerely hope it was very slight.

I was very amused to hear about Jean and her attempt to get back to England. It was quite good and fashionable. Tell her better luck next time.

There seems to be little news from this end. Alick is back to the University and Mother now all on her own. Lutterworth people keep doing away and busy as ever. I've been expecting to hear from Jimmie again but I expect he is like myself – not in very good circumstances for writing. In fact dear it's the nicest thing in the world to receive letters, but alas the replying. Don't mention it.

By the time this reaches you it will be Christmas Time. Accept my heartiest and best wishes for a Happy Xmas and prosperous New Year. Trusting you are happy and well.

With all my love. Your loving Peter.

I find it interesting that Jean was trying to get back to Britain given the War circumstances and the danger U-boats posed to all shipping even passenger liners in the Atlantic. There is an entry in Kate's address book; *"Driver J .Kemp etc., 5/201A. Army Service Company, New Zealand Force, Zeitown Camp, Egypt"*. Had Jean joined a support unit in the New Zealand Army in an attempt to get back to Britain? She was showing some ingenuity!

Peter was still in Gallipoli where conditions were extreme. The terrain was inhospitable with rocky scrub, little water, steep sided hills, deep gullies and ravines. These surroundings and close fighting did not allow for the dead to be buried. This created the perfect environment for flies and other vermin to flourish in the heat, which caused sickness in epidemic proportions. In October 1915 winter storms caused much damage and human hardship and in December a great blizzard followed by a massive thaw, resulted in 15,000 casualties throughout the British contingent *(Ref 17)*.

Arrangements were therefore made to evacuate the Peninsula and transfer the 134,000 Allies to other theatres of activity. Amazingly this evacuation was carried out in a meticulously planned and efficient way, so unlike much of what had happened before.

Thinning of troops began early and by 19 December the last man had been taken off the Suvla-Anzac sector of Gallipoli *(Ref 21a)*.

12

KATE'S HOLIDAY IN NORTH ISLAND

Summer school holidays in New Zealand were at the time of winter in Europe; circa 16 December to 26 January. In late December 1915 Kate went on a fascinating trip to Waitomo Caves, Rotorua and Auckland *(Map 7)*. Kate would have had to save quite a bit of money for this holiday. She was not accompanied by her cousin Jean. This was an organised trip.

Her thirteen page record of this has survived. Apart from her little black address book it is the only writing from New Zealand that I have from Kate. It is not a letter, more of an essay. The fact it has survived means it was not sent to Peter but kept by Kate as a memento of happy times in New Zealand. I think Peter would have had a shorter version in his letter. I have used "New Zealand A Lonely Planet Publication" *(Ref 40)* to assist with some of the names in this narrative. It may have been her last sightseeing trip in New Zealand.

We left Napier at 8.45 a.m. arriving at Palmerston North 1.30 pm, had sufficient time to lunch and see a good deal of that place. Arriving back to the station in time to catch the "Auckland – Wellington Express" to go up the main trunk line. This being our first time up this line, we found it most interesting. It was most amusing to see everyone rushing out at the different stations for cups of tea and sandwiches.

[The Auckland-Wellington Express railway line was opened in 1909. It was 424 miles long and was described as an "engineering miracle" with its viaducts, tunnels and even a spiral mechanism to make it possible for a heavy steam engine to overcome a large elevation difference. Steam trains took 20 hours to travel the 424 miles, but

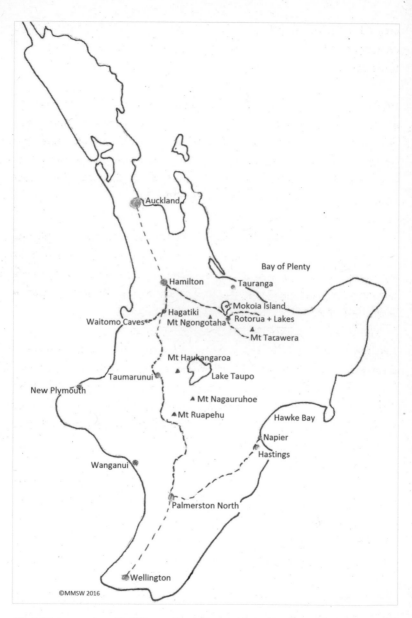

Kate's Christmas trip to The Waitomo Caves, Rotorua & Auckland December 1915 (Map 7)

created a lifeline for the young nation as it opened up the Maori central area; King Country to European settlement, investment and tourism *(Ref 70)*.]

Our next stop was at Taumarunui right in the heart of the King Country, arriving there at Midnight. We broke our journey there, and were made very comfortable at The Hotel Grand. We slept a few hours, and then set off on foot to see a bit of the place. The town is surrounded with thick bush, and we could see a glimpse of the famous Wanganui River and returned to the Hotel for breakfast.

Then took the slow train to Hangatiki (this part of the country is inhabited more with Maori's than Europeans), from there a coach conveyed us to the Government Hostel, Waitomo, a distance of six miles, through lovely country. The roads were very good, but very white. The drivers had to wear smoked glasses.

We arrived at the Hostel in time for the launch. Then had to rig up in a costume all the world like a drill tunic and wore bluchers [a type of shoe]. *The men wearing dungarees, they are kept for the use of Tourists visiting the caves. Everyone thoroughly enjoyed the dressing up. Then the Guide gave us all a lamp, and told us to follow the track, with him leading the way, (our party consisted of ten).*

We did not go far when we were met by a coach. This took us a three mile drive to the Ruakuri and Aranui Caves situated in the bush. First we did the Ruakuri, then had refreshments at a hut, kept by an old Maori Woman. Then came the Aranui, and drove back to the Hostel, had dinner. Then set off on foot to the Waitomo Cave.

These three caves are considered the most beautiful in the world. They are of limestone formation called stalactites and stalagmites. The first named are those hanging from above and the latter are those forming from the ground. They vary in colour from snow white, to a dark brown, and from every conceivable shape. Such as Brides cake, canopies, Giant's hand, Cathedral, cloisters, etc. Some are very thin, others are enormous.

The Waitomo Cave has a subterranean stream, and went up by boat keeping very quiet, and we were rewarded by seeing marvellous glow worms. This cave is done in the evening; we arrived back at the Hostel for supper and did enjoy a goodnight's rest after a strenuous day.

We left Hangatiki next day by the express, our next stop being Frankton Junction. From there we got the Rotorua express, arriving there at 5.30 pm. We have heard such a lot about the wonderland of New Zealand and were not surprised to smell the sulphur fumes, but we soon got used to that.

Our Hotel was near the Station, and it was very comfortable. After a wash and dinner, we discovered that the Hotel visitors had chartered a launch for the evening. Being moonlight, off we sailed for Mokoia Island and Hamurana Springs [Map 8 Trip a]. The first named being very well known, having a love tale attached to it. The lover's names were Hinemoa and Tutanekai. She was a lovely Maori girl, whose ancestors lived at Ohinemutu. They dwelt by the shores of the lake. As fate would have it she fell in love with Tutanekai, Maori of lowly birth. He the illegitimate son of Whankane Chief of Mokoia, and determined to fly to him. So one night she left the sleeping Pah at the sound of his flute borne across the water.

She stole down to the lake, discovered that all the canoes were drawn up high and dry, and there was no means of transit to the Island. Nothing daunted her; she procured some gourds to keep her afloat, and plunged into the water. After a 2 mile swim, she reached the Island, weary and

Kate's Rotorua trips December 1915. (Map 8)
(a) Mokoia Island and Hamurana Springs
(b) "The Round Trip" from Rotorua to Rotomahana
(c) Beautiful Lakes – Rotorua, Rotoiti, Rotoehu, Rotoma and Rotokawau.

benumbed, but a bath in the hot pool by the shores soon restored her. While she was waiting Tutanekai's slave came to fetch water for his Master, she let herself be known, asking for a drink then breaking the panuakin. The slave ran back to tell his Master what had happened. Tutanekai indignant rushed to the well, full of anger, which was changed to joy on discovering his sweetheart, and took her home to be his wife. The Maori's acted this while we were there and it made it all the more interesting.

[This love story may have made Kate think. By overcoming her difficulties Hinemoa had been reunited with her lover. But had the war changed things? Did Kate love Peter enough to keep her promise and be reunited with him? If so she had to face the risks of a long voyage home; a trip half-way round the world at a time of war. But she had a good life in New Zealand, a good job; many friends - some like Will who would do anything for her. But he was a Naval Reserve and he with many others had been called up.

She still had a lot; should she give it up and return to Britain? She could break off her engagement, marry someone else, enjoy her new life and start a family of her own. Just how much did she miss her brother Gilbert, her nieces, sisters and all the other loved ones she had left behind? What did Jean want to do? How would one be without the other? Kate had a lot to consider. Over the next twelve months she would make her momentous decision, but for now she would enjoy the adventure.]

Then came the Hamurana Springs. The way from the launch to the creek is laid out in paths and the trees are laden with cherries. When we arrived at the creek, we boarded a small boat. Not having sufficient room to use oars, the tourists had to pull themselves as best they could.

At last we reached the Springs, they are of beautiful clear water of unfathomable depth, and when we dropped coins in we could see them go over and over. It was intensely interesting to watch.

On our way back to the Launch, we gathered heaps of cherries, and had tea at a hut before returning, arriving at The Hotel at 12 p.m.

Next day we did what is known as "the round trip route" from Rotorua to Rotomahana, leaving the Hotel 8 a.m. All got a lunch basket, as there is no place to get anything to eat except a cup of tea at the Te Wairoa and Waimangu House [Map 8 Trip b].

We drove through the Tikitapu bush, went along the shores of the Tikitapu or Blue Lake. And then the green coloured Rotokakahi, through the ruined village of Te Weiroa. There we were met by a Maori Guide and he escorted us over the ruins, such as Hotels, wharves, and mission house, Te Mu. After getting our refreshments at the Hut, we continued our way by coach to the Lake Tarawera.

That is where the Eruption was in 1886 when 100 natives besides some Europeans were killed. This used to be the headquarters of the Tuhourangi tribe, which now live at Whakarewarewa, a place which I will tell you about later, but is now completely deserted of Maoris. They were tapered with so many deaths' of their people. The vegetation has now quite recovered from the effects of the volcanic deluge, and the place is thick with rich foliage.

We were then conveyed by oil launch across the Lake Tarawera, and walked over the short portage of Wiki Arm. Another launch was boarded for the Rotomahana cruise. One part of this lake is cold and the other has a tremendous hydro-thermal activity and extends into the lake a great distance. It is a steaming zone of strange sights and sounds.

The guide told us to put our hand in the water. First it was quite cold, then warmer, until boiling hot. We did think it uncanny to be sailing on a boiling lake. (This place is 30 times larger than the eruption). Then for about 2 miles the Launch skirted the geyser pitted cliffs, tinted in rainbow hue by chemical action.

The steam soaring up like smoke as we got nearer the geyser cliffs, the air became close and stuffy, and I could feel beneath the launch the thud of geysers, boiling springs surrounding us. We were then shown, by the guide, where the pink and white terraces were situated before the eruption. The heat became more, and more intense. We could hear the geysers roaring.

At last we reached the shore and were met by the Government Guide, but did not get very far, when we heard a thundering noise and were not long in discovering that it was the "Devils Blow Hole". By this time the Ladies of our party, well their nerves were a bit unstrung. It took all our courage to continue along a very dangerous path. First one wonder was shown to us, then another. All we could do was to express our astonishment, and were not sorry to get on with our journey.

By this time we reached what is known as "Frying Pan Flat", a seething mass of boiling sulphur. The Guide allowed us to walk around certain parts. We first stood on one foot then on the other. It was so terribly hot, and the fumes from the sulphur were suffocating. The place was a perfect inferno.

We saw there the great crater where the Geyser Waimangu at one time played to a height of 1000 feet. There was also a blow hole which played every 7 minutes. After spending some time there we continued our journey to Waimangu House, where a very welcome cup of tea awaited us, made by the Guide's wife.

From the Veranda we had an excellent view of Waimangu Valley, and miles of country affected by the eruption. From there we walked a little way and were rewarded by seeing a very pretty green lake. After writing our name on the "look out house", we were once more met by the coach, for our return journey of a 17 mile drive.

It was very uninteresting except for the splendid view we got of the rainbow mountain Maungakakatamea. We arrived back in Rotorua hungry and tired, but soon recovered after a good dinner and goodnight's rest to start another trip next day. This time we visited the fine beautiful lakes. Rotorua, Rotoiti, Rotoehu, Rotoma, and Rotokawau [Map 8 trip c]. This trip is done by motor car, leaving at 8 a.m.

We went along the shores of Lake Rotoehu, a romantic Lake. It is connected with Hongi's track. This is a narrow path across an isthmus, then through a belt of the richest forest in this country. The chauffeur told us many interesting tales about this park. For instance we saw the tree they used for hanging the Maori's when they committed any crime, and you may be sure it was a short one.

Hongi was a Maori chief; being ambitious he went to England. He was presented to the King and was made quite a fuss of. When he returned, he told all his people that there was only one King of England and there should be only one King of New Zealand, provided he was made King. Of course the other chiefs rebelled.

He then collected an army and they cleared this path, which took them a considerable time and waged war with the Rebels, but he was not successful, and I believe he flew the country.

Coming out of this forest we viewed Lake Rotorua with its beautiful clear blue water, with the reflection of rocky banks and shrubs. We made a stop at a hut there for tea, all having lunch baskets. Then we began our backward journey. We did not realise how dangerous the road was that we had been driving on. So engrossed were we with the beautiful scenery on our outward journey.

The road was first cut out of the bank, some places very high, and many nasty turns. We thought every minute we would land in the Lake or crash into another car. We were thankful we had a competent motorman.

Some little Maori children coming from school saw us go past and they had a lot of cherries all neatly fixed on a branch of a tree. They jumped on the bumper bar as we came back selling them for 6'and 1. (They are keen little money makers, but you can't help loving the dear little black mites). After getting a good supply of cherries, we continued our way to the Soda Springs.

They were just large pools of water and had a decided taste of soda. Just alongside was a hut where a Maori and his dog were suffocated with asphyxiating gas. It seems the Maori lost his dog and went in search and it was discovered that his hut was full of this particular gas. You may be sure that none of us cared to visit it. We will leave that stuff for the Germans.

From there we went to Lake Rotokawau, the East Lake. It was at great depth from the road not being able to get near it. But we could distinctly see wild horses on the shores, although they looked small. From there we went to Tikitere. This place is about 11 miles from Rotorua. It is a mass of boiling mud. I cannot describe the frightful sights we saw.

Well you can imagine from the name each place has, that it is uncanny. One place is called "The Inferno", a huge cauldron 23 degrees above boiling point. Just beside is "Hell's Gate", and nearby "Satan's Glory", all above boiling point. Then there are "Porridge pots", "Punch bowls", as the Maori's call them. The people say they would not be surprised if at any time Tikitere turned into one boiling crater.

We also saw for the first time a hot water fall. This being the last of the sights this trip, we drove back to Rotorua, arriving 5 p.m. After dinner we went to a Maori concert, and did enjoy seeing The Haka's and Poi dancers. They work themselves into such a trance, of course we could not understand a word and the noise was something dreadful. The next day was Xmas. (I might say the best I have ever spent in the Colonies).

After breakfast we drove to Whakarewarewa. This place is only 2 miles from Rotorua. It is a little wonderful place all on its own being so compact. On arriving there we were met by a host of Maori Guides. After choosing one, we set off to see the sights.

The first sight was a number of Maori children diving off a bridge into the river for pennies. These tiny mites spend most of their time in the water. When they get cold, they bathe in the hot pool alongside, and they would clamour around us calling in their broken English "Throw a penny". It is so amusing watching them, sometimes with as many as 9 or 10 pennies in their mouths at once.

We did not go far when we heard a whistle. This we soon learned was a warning that the Pohutu geyser was going to play (we were most fortunate every time we went to "Whaka" we saw it play). Also another called the Prince of Wales Feathers. They are a beautiful sight. The boiling water would be thrown up a great height, then fall like many diamonds.

There were several other geysers, but were not active while we were there. There were also many boiling oil and mud pools called "Porridge Pots", "Cat's Eye" and "Lily Pool" and numerous others, as they rose they form the different things. This Porridge is rather a treacherous one. It is like thick porridge boiling on a very hot stove, and makes the same noise.

Then we saw hot and cold water side by side. The Guide told us they caught trout in the one and cooked them in the other. We also saw a "brain pot" with some dreadful Maori legend attached to it. From there we were taken through a Model Maori Pah and its wonderful carving.

(That is a weakness Maori's have, everywhere you go you see carvings, and it is queer stuff).

We saw the trenches they dug when they were at war with the Europeans. It was more interesting to see the various weapons they had used in warfare. After spending some time there, the kiddies gave us a Haka for a penny. We wrote our names in the book. Then drove back to the Hotel for lunch, where great preparations were being made for the Christmas dinner.

After lunch we went to the old township of Ohinemutu [which is on the shore of Lake Rotorua]. *Only Maori's live there. They invited all Europeans to Xmas dinner mid-day. They were also entertaining the Rarotonga soldiers. This is another tribe which have volunteered for national service, and were on final leave. We did not care to have dinner with them, but it was immensely interesting watching them.*

I suppose you can hardly imagine them cooking their food in the boiling pools. (They also had plum puddings boiling).

You can also see clouds of steam rising everywhere. After watching the kiddies diving into the Lake we walked back to the Hotel to await dinner at 6 p.m. By this time the Hotel was beautifully decorated outside and in.

After we had dressed, we were surprised to hear a special band that was playing during the dinner, and all the evening on the veranda. There was also a special menu for every person and needless to say we had every good thing imaginable to eat.

After dinner we all signed our names in the different Memoirs of the Friends we had made during our stay there. We finished the evening with a dance. There were about 200 people staying at the Hotel over Xmas (1915).

Next day being Tuesday, we set off for Ohinemutu and saw a new Maori meeting house being opened. It was just like a Whare with native mats on the floor. (No seats). It was all beautifully carved. The Minister and the Elders preached a sermon in their native tongue, first on the veranda, and then we were all invited inside. We all knelt down and they prayed and that was the end.

We then visited the different churches, which like everything else was carved inside and out. We walked through the Cemetery where some of the names on the tombstones were about a mile long.

Having a few more days at Rotorua, we visited these places within easy distance, many times and spent quite a lot of our time in the Sanatorium Grounds. They are beautifully laid in flowers, tennis courts, and croquet lawns.

While the Malfroy Geysers play continuously, we saw the famous Rachel pool. The water of this pool when cool supplies the baths, one of the chief attractions of Rotorua. This pool is unfathomable and the heat of water is 160 degrees.

One night we all went for a bath. There are several swimming pools. But we preferred a private Rachel dip; the cost being a shilling for each person, with a Nurse in attendance. It was most refreshing. Our skin felt like velvet when we came out. There are various other baths for invalids only; all having different names, supposed to cure certain diseases.

A great number go there morning and night. There were quite a number of returning soldiers staying at the "San", for treatment. Coming out of the bath building we walked round the grounds, which by this time was lighted up with electricity. There was a Maori concert on the tea kiosk veranda.

It was the last night of the Rarotonga soldiers leave and they were giving Haka's and dances in aid of the local funds. They were in full Maori dress. They did look uncanny. I can tell you, they were more like animals than human beings. We thoroughly enjoyed watching their movements. That being our last night we made the most of it.

We left by the Express the next morning for Auckland arriving there at 5 p.m. On our way we saw the Ngongotaha Mountain. The Maori's think the top of this mountain is the abode of fairies or patupaiarehe and is 2554 feet high.

Auckland is more like the home cities, than any other in New Zealand (we did enjoy being in the bustle once more). It has a very pretty harbour and we visited all the different bays, having a few friends there. They gave us an excellent time betwixt motor drivers, trips across the harbour, picnicking, bathing, etc. not forgetting strawberries and cream every day and heaps of other luxuries, which are plentiful in this climate.

We had a lovely finish to our fine holiday. We left there by midnight express at 9 p.m. Being dark the journey was uninteresting until next morning when we all made a rush for a cup of tea at the famous spiral station (a miracle of engineering). Then after a short distance we viewed the snow-capped mountain - Ruapehu 9000 feet high, the highest in North Island. We also saw the Ngauruhoe another Mountain of interest.

We were rather tired by the time we reached Palmerston North. It being 12 a.m. had lunch, and caught Napier express arriving Napier 6.20 p.m. Our friends had a taxi waiting and we were not long in getting back to the school.

I have done my best to give you an idea of our holiday. Hope I have been successful. You will have to excuse my mistakes. Amen.

Sadly pictures *CP12A & PC12B* are all that survive from this adventure. What a fascinating trip. Kate was enjoying the unique beauty of North Island. Her holiday was spectacular. She was having a great time, hotel accommodation, guided tours, fine dining, everything to suit her needs and the holiday of a lifetime. What a dramatic contrast to what Peter was experiencing in Gallipoli with death and squalor around him.

Kate may have furthered her own interest in carving with what she had seen on this trip. She also liked her cups of tea!

The War was a reality for the Maori's as they joined the ANZAC contingent. Rarotonga soldiers from the Cook Islands were getting ready to take their part in the War. Returning casualties were receiving treatment at the Sanatorium in Rotorua.

Being an active volcanic island it was not surprising to discover that the original Napier School for Girls was so badly damaged in the 1931 Hawke's Bay earthquake that it had to be demolished and rebuilt.

Tourists on the "Bridge at Whaka" (PC12A)

Maori woman in costume holding ornate carving (PC12B)

13

A GREAT LOSS FOR KATE

Kate received a postcard from Mary Clarke her friend in Scotland which wished her a Merry Christmas and a Happy New Year *(PC13A)*. Sadly that was not what she experienced when she returned from her fabulous holiday.

Awaiting her was an envelope with black ink around the edge which contained a letter from Nellie, her brother's wife. Black ink surrounding an envelope meant that it contained a letter with news of a loved one's death. This practice had started in Victorian times when the death rate, especially in children, was high *(Ref 77)*.

16th Dec. 1915 Mayburn. Alloa. [This was where Nellies relatives lived. Lalla refers to them as Uncle Watson and Grandpa].
My Dear Kate,

I'd far rather talk to you than write at this time of my great sorrow. Really my heart is too sore for anything. I know ere this you will have read the sad intelligence in the papers and I also know you will be fearfully cut up. Daddy [Gilbert] *and you were always such chums that your grief will almost be equal to mine.*

This has been a terrible ordeal for me but the back is made for the burden sadly and I am fairly well but broken-hearted as you may guess. Daddy has had fearful suffering. It is ten weeks since he came home from the Hospital and it has been so much for me to nurse him. I had Aunty night and day for the last fortnight which I was very thankful for, she is a dear. Daddy was so patient all the time. I knew from the beginning there was no hope but I kept the secret and kept up my spirits for his sake till the end.

Mary Clarke's Christmas wishes to Kate 1915 (PC13A)

Nature told him at last that he couldn't get better. But it was a beautiful end and one I shall never forget. He was conscious till almost the last and said such nice things to me. It was a bitter tearing away, but he was so resigned and talked of going as if it were a holiday. I could tell you such

a lot but I have not time.

I am going down to Queen St. now. You see we drove up here on Sat. after the Funeral and have been here since. This is to be my home now, but oh dear, I am feeling home sick already, but must try to throw it off. Such is hard for me Kate, you know what sweethearts Gil and I always were. I must just look forward to meeting him again as [there is a large splurge of ink here possibly from a tear] *he said he would in the sweet "by-and-by". Shall I exist? Suppose I must for my dear girlies sake. Will tell you more next time.*

Wish you could have seen the flowers Kate and such a number too, and now I have nearly 100 beautiful letters. It is very comforting and it is lovely for me to know my dear husband has been such a general favourite.

Kate just got your parcel as I write this. Many thanks. The girls will be charmed when they come home. With much love and best wishes.

Yours always, Nellie.

What a shock for Kate. Her brother was now dead, not through war, but complications of surgery at a relatively young age; 37. She would never see him again. How would Nellie, his widowed wife cope? There would be no money to pay the rent. Nellie and her two young daughters Lalla and Nan could not remain at 21 Queen St. Shortly after Gilbert's death they had moved to "Mayburn" where John Dawson and his family lived. They were part of Nellie's extended family. There was no welfare state in 1915.

21 Queen St was cleared along with Gilbert's belongings and items left by Kate were recorded in Nellie's list given to Annie, Kate's older sister *(PC13B & PC13C).*

List of Articles now at
21 Queen St. Alloa
belonging to Catherine Bell Hay
Girls High School
Napier
Hawkes Bay
N. Zealand

1 Dressing case (small)
1. Writing Companion.
1. Jewel case.
1 Hat-pin Stand
1 pen tray - with pens
1 Small Jewel case containing small
     walnut pin cushion.
1 Small Work-box
1 Pepper (Alderley Edge) Coat of Arms.
1 Antique China plate
1. Manicure Set.
1 Photo Frame (pink silk)
1 box linen handkerchiefs.
1 handkerchief Sachet
2. Camisoles
1 Nightdress case.
1 box with Lace scarf
1. Volume Tennyson (Etta.)

A list of Kate's belongings left behind in Alloa to go to Lalla Hay if she did not return from New Zealand (PC13B)

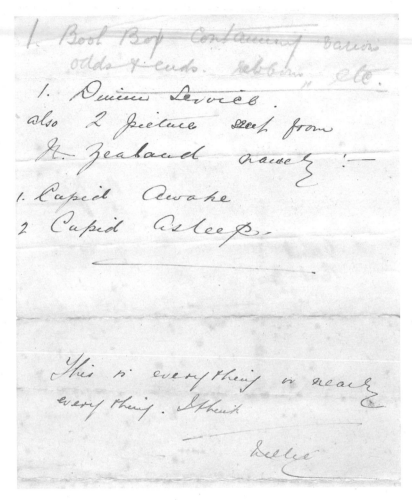

A list of Kate's belongings left behind in Alloa to go to Lalla Hay if she did not return from New Zealand (PC13C)

Kate may have felt very distant and wanted to help. She had sent money but may have yearned to get back home.

The next letter is from Annie, Kate's older sister. The envelope has a black surround to indicate bad news. There is no date but it would be early January 1916, from its content.

No 24 Ward, Royal Infirmary. Edinburgh.
My Dear Sister,

You will get a surprise when you get this letter - that I am here. I have been under the x-rays three times, but haven't had the result yet. I have been here a fortnight. I came the week after Gilbert's Funeral. The last words G. said to me were "I going away". My nerves were so strung. My mind is a little taken off it being here. I had a long letter from Nellie, I had a good sob. It always puts me back but I can't help it. You will get a dreadful shock I know. I can't realise it. I am getting some of our own mother's things, your things I suppose are going to Lalla if you don't come home (PC13B & PC13C). I feel very pleased that everything has gone off so quietly. But don't say I told you anything about your things to Nellie as it might cause trouble. Oh dear it has been a terrible time. You will have your mourning by the time you get this.

I haven't seen my good costume yet, but I know it has arrived at Tullibody, while I am here. I had Daddie and the Bairns last Monday 3rd Jan. I was pleased to see them. They were telling me they had got your books and that they were nice ones. I don't know if Rena [the youngest sister] *has written to you or not. I got the £1 all right* [about £100 in today's money *(Ref 50)*]. *I thank you very much Kate, very acceptable at a time like this.*

Well Kate I will let you know whenever I get word. Wishing you all the compliments.

Thanking you once more, your sister Annie.

Kate's immediate family were in a severe state of shock with the death of Gilbert, her nieces were without their father, and Kate loved them dearly. Kate would also be concerned that her older sister Annie was not well undergoing x-ray investigations in hospital in Edinburgh.

Nellie was taking stock after her husband's death; sorting his things out and not sure what to do with Kate's belongings that she had left behind. Annie was not even sure if Kate would come home.

14

1916 FROM SUVLA TO EGYPT TO THE SOMME

The 11th Division sailed 11 miles from Gallipoli to the Island of Imbros following the successful evacuation of Suvla 19 December 1915. It then sailed to Alexandria, Egypt arriving January 1916. The Division regrouped at Sidi Bishr in Alexandria and then took over the defence of a section of the Suez Canal. They were in position by 19 February 1916 *(Map 9) (Ref 26)*.

Peter's Brigade move from Gallipoli to guard the Suez Canal (Map 9)

At that time there was concern that the Turks relieved by the British withdrawal from Gallipoli would attack and capture the Suez Canal - the vital lifeline to India, the east coast of Africa, and the Far East. However as Turkey became under increasing threat from the Russians in the Caucasus; the threat to the Suez Canal lessened. In June the 11th Division was ordered to move to France *(Refs 21, & 30)*.

Feb.21/1916. [Unaddressed letter. This letter was probably written from the Suez Canal in Egypt.]

My Dearest Kate,

I've had such a lot of letters from you these last few days past, simply heaps of them. It is very, very kind of you to write so regularly, as I see by the date, you never miss a week. Oh if I could only say the same, however dear you understand I always have recompense in that belief.

Well Kate dear the sad news of your Brother's death came as a terrible shock the other day and I feel I must convey my heartfelt sympathy to yourself dear and also the people at home, who now mourn the loss of such an affectionate Brother.

Kate dear you must bear it all and have faith in the great unknown. Bereavement at present is such a common sorrow dear, but never lessens the individual grief and it seems that all that possibly could be done was carried out, but operations are such...

Unfortunately the letter ends here, any further pages are missing. It is possible that someone censoring this letter thought operations was to do with military matters and destroyed the rest of the letter.

Peter may have known Gilbert before he met Kate, but since his engagement to his sister they had spent time together. He too would miss him.

March 6, 1916. [Unaddressed letter. Peter was still in Egypt. It would not be until 17 June that 11th Division would be ordered back to France to reinforce the Third Army on The Somme *(Ref 30)*.]

My Dearest Kate,
I have had such a lot of correspondence from you lately, also your parcel which was very, very nice indeed. On my behalf dear please thank Miss Greig for the socks, which were A1 and very thoughtful of her indeed to think of such for your humble...

The letter ends here, any further pages are missing.

Miss Greig was playing her part in keeping Peter's feet warm; a kind practical way to show that she cared.

Violet Maude Greig MA, BSc was Head Mistress at the High School for girls in Napier from 1910 to 1926. She was a formidable woman ahead of her time; as a graduate in both art and science she could not only inspire her pupils in English language, essay and literature, but also introduced the girls to science (a male dominated subject a hundred years ago).

She even familiarised herself with shorthand and introduced it into the curriculum to improve her pupil's employment prospects during the 'Great Depression' which followed this World War.

Her stewardship through the difficult war years has been praised by pupils, staff and parents alike. Many of her girls would have lost fathers, brothers and other loved ones as New Zealand played a huge part in The War. Their distress, bewilderment and fear would have required personal care and support; much of which would have come from the teachers and staff.

Sadly the earthquake of 3 February 1931 which demolished the school also destroyed early records that relate to this period in the school's history *(Ref 5)*.

April 16th 1916. [Unaddressed letter.]
My Dearest Kate

Haven't had any letters these last two mails, however I expect better luck next one. How are you after your fall dear? Cheer O and let's know you are your old self again, and benefited by your holiday.

I had a letter from home the other day. Mother was saying Alick was home for Easter and expected to be able to finish the ensuing term. Jimmy is still making munitions at Gorton near Manchester. The receiving of this letter, necessitated my writing to John, congratulating the household in the addition to the family, a little girl (PC14A). My word Kate they haven't lost much time, have they?

From all accounts John is likely to be called up very shortly in the first batch of married groups. That may be inconvenient, but only tends to keep one's "Thinker" in order.

In a letter from Lutterworth, Mrs D. was saying all the workmen had been starred, so that's so much to their advantage [this refers to the practice of stars being worn by men working in factories to sustain the war effort ensuring they were not mislabelled as cowards. Conscription was introduced on 2 March 1916. Initially it applied to unmarried men between 18 and 41, but soon married men were included *(Ref 47)*].

Peter's Mother Mary Wardlaw holding her first Granddaughter Margaret Young Wardlaw born 26 March 1016 (PC14A)

How are things at Queen St. since Gil's death? I feel so sorry in that line and at times think the less able are to stand the greatest strain.

I had a letter from Mary Clarke written from Glasgow. She seems to be

*fairly well satisfied with her new post but says W.D.F. her old boss of 166
Buchannan St. isn't in any way settled yet.*

Keeps very warm here. Storms of sand very frequent and annoying.

*Must stop now dear, trusting you are well and with fondest love,
Your loving Peter.*

Peter was not aware that Gilbert's widow Nellie and the two girls
were required to move out of their family home.

Climate conditions in Egypt were irritating Peter; desert, intense heat
and sand storms.

Peter mentions Miss Clarke who had helped him find the place in
Glasgow to repair the bowls. They had later gone to the Empire. A
far cry from what he was experiencing in the Army. She had lost her
job as her employer Mr Forbes' business collapsed. Some businesses
thrived as war consumed their products while others which were
successful in peacetime died.

On 1 May 1916 Peter was give the Commission of Second Lieutenant
in the Royal Field Artillery *(Refs 41 & 56. PC14B)*. His Division left
Alexandria in Egypt on 3 July 1916 for France *(Ref 30)*.

The next letter is from Lalla Hay, Kate's niece.

*29.8.16. Mayburn. Alloa.
Dear Aunt Kate,
I must set to and answer your letter. Thank you so much for the many
presents I have not yet had time to thank you for. First about Jumper and
Skirt. The skirt is to be made into a petticoat for me. And Jumper fits*

Campaign :—

1914-15

(A) Where decoration was earned.

(B) Present situation.

	Name	Corps	Rank	Reg. No.	Roll on which included (if any)		
(A)	WARDL~A~EW	RFA	Sjt	10626	VIC RFA OFF 132 270		
					BRITISH do do		
(B)	Peter H.	—1—	2ⁿᵈ Lt X		15 STAR RFA/1AB 1140		

15. Star returned.   C.R.V. 59. 2/7.10.20. 27/4/2756.   Commn 4/5/16
Action taken

1915 Star.   O/2 R+F Roll RFA/330³—46705
B. W4V. M.   IV.X/8278 df 2-3-22   EF/8/6106

Surname amended   Min. 14: E.F/8/6106.

THEATRE OF WAR (3) Egypt

Lieut/Roll qualble 24/6/19 — 9-1-7-14   Badge 23039 8 df 20/8/19   136758/9

1. 7. 15   E.F/9/3693.

QUALIFYING DATE

(6 34 16) W234—HP5590   500,000   4/19 HWV(P240)   K608   E7/8/6106   [OVER.

Correspondence

Roll submitted by O/C R.&F.A. Recs Woolwich —
at Comm: men. 6.8.50.

Extract from E7/9/3693. 8/4/20.

O.I/c Recs. RA+R.F.A. return 15 Star. owing to subsequent Commn
E79 red? 21/10/21

Address. C/o H. E. Palmer
29, New Bridge St.
London EC4

Peter's war record promotion to Lieutenant three campaigns and medals
The 1915 Star was returned due to his subsequent commission (PC14B)

Nan to a T. Also many thanks for Egyptian views which we received last night. I was ill for two days but I am well again.

I am writing in a scorching sun in the back green. I have got a bike and have learnt to ride it, so I have some fun with it, only it is too hot today.

We have got a little Pussy called Tammy. We did not know whether to call it Hay or Dawson, so we decided on "Thomas Mayburn" and sometimes for fun "The Rev John". It is a dear little thing. Nan has it and a doll in her pram just now. The hens are annoying me with their clock, clock clocooing.

We are having friends from Stirling tomorrow. We had Aunt Chris for 10 days and at some time Aunt Flo and Alistair from Barrow in Furnace for a week, so Mumma had a time of it.

This is washing day. I don't know if I ever told you of my success in music. I passed with Honours and I got 2nd Merit at school. I will try for the Dux medal (which I have a chance of next year), and also I will try for a Paton Bursary. I was trying for it this year but it meant that I would have to skip the 6th and that would never do.

Uncle John was at Edinburgh a week and we had a most enjoyable holiday at Glenfarg. Uncle Watson and Grandpa are away just now at Ayr.

Do please tell Jean that I should have written in answer to the post card, but will do soon.

Thomas Mayburn is getting a row from Nan just now. I have been down the town this morning so I have been busy. Aunt Chris is getting on splendid at Glasgow and likes it. I just wish you were home. We congratulate Jean on her success. Here comes Uncle John and he will be reading what I am writing so I will stop. Trusting you are well.

Yours aye. Lalla.

P.S. Thomas Mayburn sends his love, and please excuse my hurried scribbles.

Lalla was growing up faster than Kate could imagine. Her Aunt's gift of a jumper was too small but it did fit her younger sister. Lalla would soon be in the senior school. I am sure Kate would have loved to see her nieces again. It was almost five years since she had made up her mind to go to New Zealand. She would soon be making firm plans to make the long voyage home.

Peter's presents from Egypt were making their way to Alloa.

It is likely that the picture of Peter's mother Mary, with her first granddaughter Margaret was sent directly from Alloa keeping Kate up-to-date with family news; sharing her joy with her future daughter-in-law.

I do not know what success Jean was to be congratulated for, but she did get married in New Zealand.

The Paton Bursary mentioned was aimed at helping brighter children reach their goal in education. John Paton had set up a yarn-spinning business in Alloa which became established at Kilncraigs Mill and later combined with Baldwin's to become the world famous Paton and Baldwin's Limited *(Ref 63)*.

Around this time Kate would have been aware in New Zealand of the information printed 20 August 1916 in the New York Times, "New Steamship service through Panama canal from Wellington, New Zealand, to London was inaugurated when the steamer Remuera of the New Zealand Shipping Company passed through the canal last month en route to London". Prior to this her voyage back would have been round Cape Horn through the notorious Drake Passage *(Ref 4)*.

On 3 July 1916, three days after the Battle on The Somme started, the 11th Division departed from Alexandria in Egypt being among the last units to leave. They disembarked at Marseille on the Mediterranean coast of France. After travelling overland Headquarters were set up in Flesselles and by 27 July they were in the front line on The Somme *(Refs 30 & 31)*.

15

1916 THE SOMME

The First Day of The Battle of The Somme was Saturday 1 July 1916 *(Map 10)*. The initial attack focused on Thiepval, a village situated in the middle of The Front on a ridge high above the Ancre River, which is a tributary of the Somme. It commanded the highest ground for miles around the village and therefore was of vital strategic importance. Unfortunately it was in German hands. The Germans had turned it into a fortress with an interlocking network of blockhouses, concealed machine guns in reinforced concrete shelters and heaps of barbed wire all along their side of The Front.

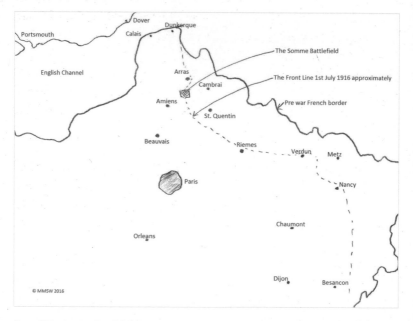

Site of The Somme Battlefield
(Map 10)

Below ground the Germans had constructed a strong network of shell proof bunkers, and dugouts, some of which were thirty feet deep; here were their headquarters with many different facilities; even the luxury of baths for the soldiers.

After a massive artillery barrage, and the explosion of mine chambers, the infantry, certain of success moved out of their trenches into the illusion of an empty battlefield. What happened next has shocked the world ever since *(Refs 7, 21b, 32, 33, 34, 42, 43, 45, 47a & 48)*.

There are numerous descriptions of what happen; barbed wire had not been cut, German defenders suddenly appeared, machine guns fired, the British creeping barrage passed beyond, the attacking infantry was met with frenzied fire; there was massacre in the barbed wire and shell holes of no-mans-land. The advance withered away. The slaughter was immense.

On this day of the 100,000 men who entered no man's land 20,000 were dead and 40,000 were wounded. This was just the start of ever increasing human sacrifice to gain small territorial advantages on The Somme in the summer and autumn of 1916.

It was to this theatre of action that Peter's 58th Brigade, Royal Field Artillery, 11th Northern Division had been transferred from Egypt. They were to reinforce the area held by the Third Army on The Somme and would take part in the battles that followed *(Refs 11 & 30)*.

Peter had been promoted to the rank of 2nd Lieutenant on 1 May 1916 when in Egypt *(Ref 41)*. He was now in command of two gun sections. I presume that this would be 'A' battery 58th Brigade RFA. The Artillery was gaining both in experience and technique. A lot would have been demanded of Peter as a Gunnery Officer. He would have had to use the network of triangulated points on maps built up from photographic images, many of them taken by reconnaissance aeroplanes in the process referred to as Ordinance Surveying. He could then identify the exact location of targets to hit. This technique, "predicted fire" could then surprise the enemy *(Ref 21c)*.

He would also have been familiar with the creeping barrage; the movement of a line of exploding shells just in front of a line of advancing infantry. This would have been a very difficult skill. Communication with the infantry was often poor in a battle zone. Telephone lines often failed as they were destroyed in bombardments. There was no tactical radio contact, a development of the future - the artillery had to fire by timetable, calculated by the speed at which the infantry was expected to advance.

In practice, because the artillery feared killing its own infantry, the intervals in distance between lifts were made too long, with the result that the attacking waves of infantry would see the barrage creeping away in front of them, beyond the trenches still strongly held by the enemy. With no means of calling the Artillery back, they were then on their own. Confidence in a creeping barrage was misplaced *(Ref 7 & 47)*.

Other areas of involvement for Peter would be counter-battery fire, with "flash spotters" identifying the sites of enemy batteries for his gun crews to neutralise *(Refs 29 & 21c)*. The enemy of course would hope to do likewise.

By September 1916 battles on The Somme were raging and the 11th Division was in the thick of it.

The 58th Brigade provided Artillery support for the Infantry of the 11th Division in the Capture of the Wundt-Werk on 14 September and again it was involved in the battle of Flers-Courcellette and the capture of Martinpuich between 15 and 22 September 1916. Tanks were used for the first time in this battle. The average advance on the six mile front was one mile. Although the tank had an initial damaging effect on German morale mechanical problems readily put them out of action *(Refs 30, 33 & 47)*. Soon after this battle Thiepval would be next.

20 September 1916. [Unaddressed letter. Written from The Somme.]
My Dearest Kate,

Time keeps rolling on and not much change, only the weather is showing the signs of fast approaching winter. To you dear it will be summer. Your last letter seemed full of anxiety to go to the U.S.A. Really I don't think it is much to be envied going there. Life is so much different to the colonies and opportunities do not appear in the same sphere at all.

However dear, I don't have the experience to talk on the subject, only that's how it all appears to me.

Oh yes I would much like to see your carving and hope to hear of your persevering with it. There's no knowing Kate, a lot of practice and the hobby will again be most fascinating.

Mother is at Lutterworth and has been there for 3 weeks now. From all reports Lutterworth has proved an attraction now. Jim from Manchester is a regular visitor, and I suppose Alick from Crystal Palace will be another addition to the list. There's only the Bellevue people now and all the Wardlaw's will have been callers.

Latest news from Alick finds him in fairly good humour and I believe a few of his "Varsity" pals who were there in advance, made his arrival a really good welcome even though the time was 1 a.m.

I am looking forward to having a leave in the near future, all being well, it's now approx. 15 months since we sailed for the Dardanelles. However dear, I suppose our turn will come shortly. Must stop now dear, glad to know you are well. With all kind thoughts,

Your loving Peter.

This letter suggests that Kate was seriously considering a voyage to America and asks Peter what he thought about staying there before it became safer to return to Britain. Peter had been away for a considerable time with no leave to return to Britain in fifteen months. He was hoping his time would come soon.

There is no mention in this or further letters of Peter's promotion. Presumably he was not permitted to tell her about this. As an Officer he would now be censoring soldiers' letters for any comments that could help the enemy. He may have been trying to tell Kate indirectly that Alick was now in The Royal Navy.

Before the First World War Crystal Palace in London was an exhibition centre. After the War started it was used as a naval training establishment under the name of HMS Victory V1, informally known as HMS Crystal Palace. Men in the Royal Naval Volunteer Reserve and other Royal Naval services were trained for war at Crystal Palace. Alick's "Varsity" pals, like him, may have been Naval Reservists *(Ref 68)*.

Jimmie was involved with munitions as an engineer with gunnery experience from the battlefield. He could provide feedback on practical issues to the factories that produced munitions based in Gorton Manchester.

John's address was *'Bellevue'*; he was the only brother who had not yet joined up. Was Peter trying to let Kate know about his brothers' war effort without breaking censorship?

21 September 1916. [Unaddressed letter. Probably written during a break in the Battle of Fleurs-Courcellette.]
My Dearest Kate,

I have just received your parcel and letter of July 2nd and take this opportunity of acknowledgment. Time is so jolly awkward now Kate for writing. I much appreciate the thoughtfulness of your people at home dear in their remembrances of my welfare.

It takes me all my time dear to remember Mary Troop, in fact I'm really guessing to say I do.

Mother extended her stay at Lutterworth and is enjoying her holiday a treat. Excuse this scrawl Kate dear but I've just taken an opportunity for a scribble. Good luck and all my love.

Your loving Peter.

There were no other letters in the ornate wooden box written by Peter from The Somme. He may have written others, but if there were any they either did not reach Kate or she did not keep them. The next letter in my possession is dated July 1917.

Certain major events for both of them took place in the intervening ten months. The unusual ending to his letter wishing Kate good luck may be an indication that he was well aware of her intention to endure the dangers of a sea voyage.

On The Somme between July and late September 1916, the British Artillery guns and howitzers fired more than seven million shells and the German Army suffered. Attrition was working, grinding down the German Army *(Ref 21b)*.

After such a long separation was Peter's love for Kate fading into a distant memory? Yes her bundles of letters lifted his mood and reminded him that there was normal life being lived out somewhere; he had not seen, or been part of that for a long time. He yearned for leave to taste some normality again. Could he still relate to the innocence in Kate's letters, with her joy in wood carving, socialising and travelling to exciting places?

Here he was surrounded by graphic images of war. There was no hiding from it. Death and destruction on a massive scale; with fear, mutilation, agony, squalor, constant noise and the all-pervasive smells of death and decay detaching men from humanity. The futility of it all as comrades died for a few muddy feet of ground. Here he was trying to write. Desperate to keep in touch with *"his Dearest Kate"* but not able to find the words, he states *"time is jolly awkward for writing"*. The Somme Battlefield was relentlessly grinding him down.

He was an officer in command; responsible for sixty men and the deployment of two 18 pound field guns. There was no room for sentiment or emotion when duty and survival required an iron resolve.

By late September the British Commander in Chief Douglas Haig had instructed General Gough, Commander of the Fifth Army (previously known as the Reserve Army) to conduct a further attack on Thiepval to avenge the disaster of 1 July . After a massive artillery bombardment lasting three days and nights, during which over a hundred thousand shells, including gas had poured into the Thiepval

Ridge, the advance began on Tuesday 26 September *(Map 11)*.

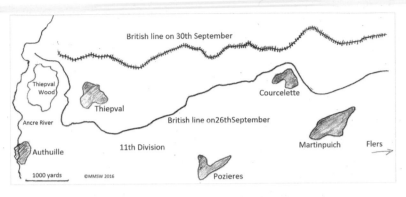

Small territorial gains made on The Somme September 1916 (Map 11).

The 11th Northern Division with its attached Royal Artillery took part in the savage fighting which achieved its objective in capturing the Ridge; however it suffered 3615 casualties *(Ref 32)*. This means that if the division strength was fifteen thousand men, the resulting casualty rate of 24 percent represents a massive loss. Peter would have known many of these men as friends and comrades.

He had already experienced the horror of Gallipoli, now he was a witness to the abhorrence of The Somme. It would have a profound effect on him. Small territorial gains were made with enormous sacrifice.

My maternal grandfather, Guardsman Tom Stirrat of the 2nd Battalion Scots Guards, would never mention what he had witnessed in the War. Perhaps this was his way of sparing us from the horror, or his way of coping with what he had seen and been part of. He joined the Scots Guards in August 1914, following family tradition. He was involved in many battles on the Western Front. As a child he told me that he had often been the only one in his platoon to have survived when they went "over the top". He had lost many friends and comrades. He had shrapnel wounds to his skull, back and hip but this did not stop his service to King and Country to the end of the War and beyond. Such scars would be nothing compared to the mental trauma he endured. These scars were carried throughout his long life. In conversation he declared himself to be a "fatalist" - could he ever believe there was a God? My Grandfather was 85 when he died.

October and November 1916 brought little gains, and increasingly wet weather turned the chalky surface of The Somme battlefield into a glutinous slime. The Allied offensive officially came to a halt on 19 November 1916. The line of advance was only seven miles from where it had started on 1 July 1916.

The Germans had suffered 600,000 casualties: men killed or wounded, to keep their position on The Somme. The Allies had lost over 600,000. The French casualty figure was 194,451 and the British 419,654. It was the greatest tragedy in all of Britain's military history. So many deaths were among the Pals and Chums Battalions who so readily joined up to protect King and Country. There was innocence; even a naivety then that was soon shattered *(Refs 7,21b, 32, 33, 42, 43, 45, 47a & 47b)*.

By 14 December 1916 Kate had a New Zealand passport *(PC15A)*. She had made up her mind to return to Britain.

DESCRIPTION OF BEARER.

Age 2 7 Profession *Spinster*

Place & date of birth / *Alloa, Scotland*
                        9th November 1889

Maiden name if widow or
married woman travelling
singly

Height 5 feet 5 inches

Forehead *High*   Eyes *Dark Brown*

Nose *Straight*   Mouth *Full*
                  Lower Lips

Chin *Round* Colour of Hair *Dark Brown*

Complexion *Slightly Sallow* Face *Oval*

Any special peculiarities *None*

National Status *Natural Born*
                British Subject

Kate's passport. Her date of birth should state 1888 not 1889.
(PC15A)

16

KATE RETURNS TO BRITAIN

On 19 February 1917 Kate and Jean were in New York *(PC16A)*. They would probably have left Napier in December, sometime after the summer holidays started in mid-December. They may have visited the beautiful subtropical Pitcairn Island; famous for "The Mutiny on the Bounty" in 1789. This was a regular stop for the SS Remuera 3435 miles from New Zealand as she crossed the Pacific Ocean to the Panama Canal *(Ref 4)*; then up the east coast of America to New York. The total distance of this voyage was some 9000 miles; a trip that had been made regularly by the SS Remuera since July 1916 *(Map 12)*.

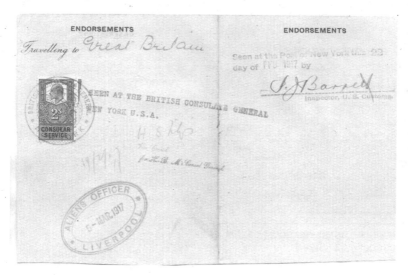

Passport stamps - departures and arrivals (PC16A)

On 22 February 1917 Kate and Jean left New York for Liverpool. They may have thought that a passenger liner from America would be safer than sailing directly to Britain. America had not yet declared

World Map - Kate's trip back to Britain (Map 12)

war, so U-boat attack would be less likely on boats from America carrying passengers from the States.

Kate and Jean returned to Britain on the SS Andania *(PC16B)*. This ship was owned by Cunard. She had been built in Greenock in 1913, could transport over 2000 passengers and travel at a speed of 15 knots per hour. Earlier in the War she had been used as a Troop Ship, transporting Canadian soldiers across the Atlantic to Europe, and in 1915 Irish Fusiliers to the shores of the Mediterranean to take part in the Suvla Bay landing in Gallipoli *(Ref 37 & 38)*.

In 1917 the SS Andania was running a transatlantic service between New York and Liverpool. Kate and Jean are the only two passengers from New Zealand registered in the record of incoming passengers. Jean is recorded in her married name; Jeannie Allan. Their "Country of Intended Future Permanent Residence" is recorded as Scotland *(Ref 39)*.

Kate and Jean crossed the Atlantic on the SS Andania (Ref 39 Passenger List) New York 22 February 1917 to Liverpool 5 March 1917 Kate's passport is stamped by the 'Aliens Officer' (PC16B)

I would conclude that they did not intend to return to New Zealand.

Kate had left so much behind: an excellent job in a popular school that recognised her ability and had rewarded her accordingly, a network of friends and colleagues, and the beauty of the countryside where she had travelled, learned to horse ride and developed an interest in wood carving. She would take with her the satisfaction that she had achieved all this. Now she was on her way home with her cousin Jean. What stories they would have to tell.

Jean had married a sailor in the Royal Navy, Frank Allan, and hoped to live with him in his home town, Plymouth. Kate would be looking forward to meeting up with Peter her fiancé at his brother Jimmie's wedding in April when she hoped he would be on leave from France. Both women would be hoping and praying that they would all be spared to enjoy normal married life in the future. The War would have to end soon.

There would have been much emotion tempered by fear as they approached the waters around Ireland where almost two years ago the Lusitania had been sunk with so much loss of life. Would they make it to Liverpool?

But Kate and Jean were a lucky pair. They had made two long sea voyages; in total about 22,000 miles. They had left Britain in February 1912 sailing the Atlantic Ocean, down to Cape Horn at the southern tip of South America into the Pacific Ocean and on to New Zealand *(Ref 4)*. Then in December 1916 they set off across the Pacific Ocean to the Panama Canal and up the east coast of North America to New York *(Ref 4)*. From New York they crossed the Atlantic to arrive in Liverpool. This was quite an achievement for two young women at this time in history.

It is of interest that the SS Andania was sunk twelve months later off the coast of Ireland on 27 January 1918 by a torpedo from the German submarine, "U-46" *(Ref 37 & 38)*.

In February 1917 Peter's Artillery Brigade as part of the 11th Northern Division was involved in the support of a successful infantry attack to capture high ground north of the Ancre River. This forced the Germans to retreat and gave British forces a commanding position for future offensives *(Ref 47b)*. It would have been after this event that Peter was granted leave from the Western Front, almost two years since he sailed for Gallipoli.

On 3 March 1917 Kate arrived in Liverpool. She had returned to fulfil her promise to Peter. Five years previously they had both made promises to be true to one another whatever happened. They could never have imagined that war would prolong their separation.

Peter and Kate may have met up at some stage before the wedding. There is no way of knowing how long Peter was allowed as leave, but they were both present at his brother Jimmie's wedding to Catherine Fyfe Cook *(PC16C)* on 7 April 1917. Peter signs the register as a witness to his brother's marriage.

It is interesting that the Registrar who records the information is Annie M Wardlaw, and she underlines her signature as a witness. She is Peter's Aunt, his late father's younger sister, born in 1870.

Catherine Fyfe Cook 1895 - 1988 Married James Taylor Wardlaw 6 April 1917 (PC16C)

Kate and Catherine Wardlaw (nee Cook) would remain close friends throughout their lives. To my Father she was always Aunt Kate, and he continued his friendship long after his Mother had died. I did meet Aunt Kate Wardlaw in person. She was a lovely lady who lived to the grand old age of ninety three. If only I had asked her more about her life. She was the only relative I ever met who had lived through the turmoil enclosed in these pages. She may also have been able to cast some light on the reunion between her future brother-in-law and Kate, and the story that was to follow.

The wedding was probably a happy time, a marked contrast to the fear, death and destruction of war.

Soon after the wedding Peter returned to the Western Front to take part in the June offensive. Kate, I presume, was in Alloa with her relatives. There is nothing to suggest at this stage that there were any issues between her and Peter, though it would have been an interesting reunion. They had spent the last five years apart and had been engaged through Peter's written request soon after she arrived in New Zealand. She had his engagement ring and she wore it.

They had sustained each other through the cruellest, gruelling and unpredictable times of anyone's lives. They were together again, but only for a short time. It was during this momentous reunion with caution thrown to the wind and passion heightened that my father was conceived.

Now Peter was in more danger, as he headed for Flanders to join the Second Army's massive offensive on the Armentieres - Ypres Front *(Ref 21d)*. The Battle of Messines was about to begin.

17

ALICK'S CONTRIBUTION TO THE WAR EFFORT

Did anyone at the wedding know that Alick would see active service the following month? He had joined the Royal Naval Volunteer Reserve at some stage. Peter mentions in his letter of 31 August 1915, *"Alick is on a boat for the August month just to keep him out of mischief"*. There is also another letter that mentioned him being on a boat on the Clyde in 1916. Peter also states in his letter of 20 September 1916 that Alick had been to Crystal Palace. This was where the Navy trained the Reserves.

There may have been a family connection with the Royal Navy as previously mentioned; the first "Q" ship success was in July 1915 when Lieutenant Mark Wardlaw surprised and sank a submarine. In May 1917, Able Seaman Alick Wardlaw is recorded as an Ordinary Telegraphist on the HMS Paxton *(Ref 22)*.

The HMS Paxton was built by the Ardrossan Dockyard and Shipbuilding Co Ltd and was launched in 1916 as the Lady Patricia for use by the British Steam and Packet Company. However she was requisitioned by the Royal Navy and converted to a "Q" ship between March and the end of April 1917, and started her service on 1 May 1917 *(Ref 22)*.

HMS Paxton was in the Atlantic Ocean ninety miles west of Great Skellig, off the coast of Ireland on the morning of Sunday 20 May when an unknown German submarine attacked. The Paxton fired back revealing herself as a "Q" ship. The submarine dived to escape *(Ref 22)*.

The Paxton headed westwards and the crew tried to disguise its identity by painting the name of a Swedish ship on her side. Later in the evening of the same day she was attacked by the submarine "U-46". Two torpedoes were fired at HMS Paxton disabling her engine and breaking her back. She sank in just a few minutes. Two Sailors were killed. The surviving crew were able to get onto life boats; but they were not able to send out a distress message for help *(Ref 22)*.

The submarine surfaced and took the Captain and second engineer prisoner. The rest were at the mercy of the Atlantic. Fortunately for most of the remaining crew they were spotted by the USS Wadsworth, an American destroyer and another ship that came to their rescue. However one of the life boats was not spotted and took several days to reach land. Provisions and water had run out and two of the crew were dead *(Ref 22)*. One of these two was Alick. My father told me that relatives advised him that if Alick had not drank sea water he would probably have survived like the others on the life boat. How sad.

Alick's war records state that no body was found *(Ref 49)*. The Atlantic had claimed him. His mother, my great grandmother, had lost her youngest son and could not give him a burial. He was twenty one years of age and was just about to complete his Honours Degree in Engineering at Glasgow University. He had joined up like his older brothers to serve King and Country. Such a tragic waste; so typical of that time *(PC17A & PC17B)*.

The Commander of the submarine "U-46" was Leo Hillebrand. He was just doing what his country required of him. It was either his submarine or HMS Paxton. In war are there any humane options? During World War One this submarine was responsible for sinking 52 ships, 140,314 tons. Almost all of these vessels were sunk off the west coast of Great Britain *(Ref 72)*.

Alexander (Alick) Gillespie Wardlaw born 1896 Studied Engineering at Glasgow University 1914-1917. Joined the Royal Naval Volunteer Reserve summer of 1915 Telegraphist on the "Q" Ship HMS Paxton which was torpedoed.
Died 20 May 1917 aged 21
(PC17A)

WARDLAW, Ord. Tel. Alexander Gillespie, Clyde/Z/8170. R.N.V.R. H.M.S. " Paxton." Killed in action with submarine in Atlantic 20th May, 1917. Age 21. Son of James Taylor Wardlaw and Mary Hutchison Wardlaw, of Alloa, Clackmannanshire. Student of Glasgow University. 28.

Extract from newspaper June 1917 (PC17B)

It is a strange coincidence that "U-46" was the same submarine patrolling off the coast of Ireland in January 1918 that torpedoed and sunk the SS Andania; the ship that had brought Kate and Jean safely back to Britain.

18

1917 THE BATTLE OF MESSINES

On the Western Front *(Map 13)*, The French Army under General Neville carried out an attack called "Rupture". It was in the Southern Aisne sector at Chemin Des Dames, an area that in previous times had been beautifully landscaped for the pleasure of Louis XV's daughters. Here the French Army opened its attack on 16 April 1917 against heavily defended German defences. The result was a catastrophe with 29,000 killed, losses that could not be replaced. The French Army was in crisis. Mutiny followed and General Neville was replaced by General Petain. The subversion was put down by court–martial, firing squad and imprisonment *(Refs 7, 44 & 47c)*.

With the demoralised French Army in crisis, the Anglo-French strategy for 1917 was in tatters. New plans were needed. British and Colonial Divisions making up The Second Army would attack the German front line at Messines. This would force the Germans to move reserves from the Arras and Aisne fronts, to reinforce their Flanders line, and in so doing relieve pressure on the French *(Refs 7 & 35)*.

The first phase of General Haig's Flanders offensive began at the end of May 1917 with a series of massive bombardments. The Second Army was under the command of General Plumer who had built up a reputation for meticulous planning and preparation. The Infantry worked well with the Artillery *(Ref 29)*.

In May three Divisions, including the 11th Division with the attached 58th Brigade of the Royal Field Artillery were moved north from Arras to become reserve divisions for those corps in the Second

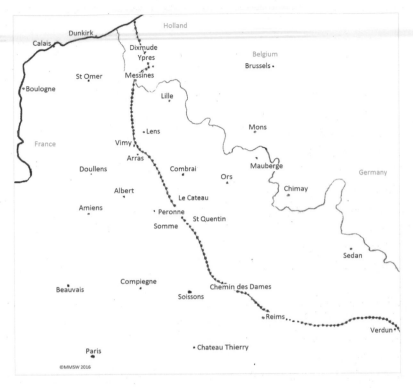

Western Front with site of Messines Battlefield (Map 13)

Army that were preparing to attack the Messines Ridge. They then took part in the forthcoming battle *(Ref 35)*.

Following a massive preliminary bombardment against the German positions on the Armentieres-Ypres front, the Battle of Messines started on 7 June 1917. The ultimate aim of Haig's offensive was to clear the Belgian coast, eliminate the submarine bases at Zeebrugge and Ostend, and force a German withdrawal from northern Belgium. The capture of Messines-Wytschaete Ridge, taken by the Germans at the end of October 1914, would give the British an advantage for the next step in the attack planned for Ypres.

Over the previous two years British Royal Engineers had been digging deep mines under the German lines and packing them with explosives. The attack was massive both above and below ground. The explosion of nineteen huge mines, containing 500 tons of high-explosive, on the morning of 7 June, signalled the infantry attack.

The devastating effect of exploding mines surprised and shocked the German defenders, while the attacking infantry were supported by tanks, overhead machine gun fire, gas bombardment and burning oil drums *(Refs 7, 18, 21d, 35, 45 & 47d)*.

Peter may have written letters from Messines when he returned to the battle zone but there were none in Kate's ornate wooden box.

Here was Peter on the front line, very close to the enemy in command of his Gun Battery; responsible for his own men but also to the infantry providing supporting fire from his gun crew. Would his mind not have drifted to the wedding where he and his sweetheart had thrown caution to the wind intoxicated in the pleasure of their reunion? He had fallen in love with Kate as a young businessman six years ago. In his eyes she had given him so much luck. But he was now a military man. As Commanding Officer he had responsibility; emotions had to be contained, there was no room for sentiment. He must focus as the battle commenced.

The field artillery batteries of the three reserve divisions which included the 58th Brigade were in camouflaged positions, close to the British front line. Peter's Battery would have been in place ready to support the Infantry in the next phase of the attack. The infantry readily achieved its initial objective with fewer casualties than expected; this resulted in congestion on the ridge making them easy targets for the Germans. As they gathered for the next phase of the attack the Germans opened fire with machine-guns and artillery. The camouflaged batteries of the reserve divisions returned fire, but in doing so revealed their position to the enemy *(Ref 35)*.

The attack was a complete success, and the Germans were forced back, withdrawing to suitable defensive positions.

At some stage during this battle Peter's luck ran out and he became a casualty. My father told me that he was buried alive. He had to be dug out and lost his leg. He was probably hit by German counter battery fire. He would have received treatment in a field hospital just behind the front line and when stable, shipped back to Britain.

The next letter from Peter is from Roehampton Hospital, where he was having a "prosthetic" leg fitted. He would have been aware by this time that his youngest brother Alick was dead. Kate had also written to him in his convalescence with the news that she was pregnant.

19

TOGETHER AGAIN?

The Battle of Messines lasted from 7 to 14 June. Peter was a war casualty, he had lost his leg. By the end of July, some six weeks later, he was learning to walk again with an artificial limb; physically he was making good progress. However, while coping with mutilation he also faced the bitter sadness of his brother's death and the prospect of fatherhood now that his Fiancée was pregnant.

28.7.17 Dover House, Roehampton.S.W. (PC19A)
My Dearest Kate,
I've just received yours. Oh yes, I had a letter from Jean. Of course I assume you are keeping the matter between yourselves. Now Kate if you think you would be more comfortable, in say a boarding house, which are ok in Blackpool, or even a Hotel, so as to treat life more as a holiday, for a time until I know how I am to be placed.

I expect my leg on Tuesday (31.7.17) and will be leaving here a week later, by then I will have had my board and will likely know how I am to be placed regarding the Army. Personally I'm afraid I won't obtain my release. Anyhow Kate we can be married after I leave here with my leg, but we won't say much about it until nearer the time. I should stay in London or somewhere anyhow we won't trouble anybody to come to it.

I will write Mother in about a week, but I am not having anyone present. I know she will be asking why, but I won't enlighten her or any other body. So Kate I shouldn't write north for a bit. If we are married in a hurry they can be told afterwards.

I was in London the other day and was seeing two small cars, but up till now I haven't decided on either.

Thank Jean for her letter which was very kind of her. I am rather anxious on seeing Jean to have a talk. Is she comfortable where she is? Because if not and she is agreeable to having a holiday with you for say a fortnight, I shall be pleased to stand good for same.

Will write you again in a day or so Kate.

With fondest love, and all good wishes. Peter.

Exterior View of Queen Mary's Convalescent Auxiliary Hospital in Roehampton showing main entrance and drive, 1914-18. Red Cross archives 1447/IN2188 (Ref 64). (PC19A)

Was it kind and thoughtful of Peter to pay for Kate and Jean to have a holiday in Blackpool?

Would he not have felt that she needed him now that she was pregnant? And would it not have been more appropriate to have his *"Dearest Kate"* close by to help him through this ordeal? Or did he want to keep her at a distance until he had dealt with his immediate situation such as coming to terms with his artificial leg, learning to walk again and what the Army would do with him; he had worked tirelessly, dedicating everything to King and Country over the last three years. His endeavours had been rewarded in the previous year with a commission. He was Lieutenant Peter Wardlaw, but what would the Army now want of him?

Did he not need time and space to deal with his other issues? The woman that had captivated him over six years ago, that he had fallen in love with, who wore his ring, and had lifted his mood in the trenches when her bundles of letters arrived; his *"Dearest Kate"*, had now come back for him. She was also pregnant with his child following their re-union. Did he still love her?

Peter does not appear to be pleased with the pregnancy. It would seem to be an accident in his eyes. He realises he must do the right thing for that period in time and get married. Perhaps because of the sadness in Alloa after his brother's death, or his surprise at being confronted with Kate's pregnancy, he does not want anyone at their wedding and he does not want Alloa to know their business.

Was he ashamed or embarrassed? He had expressed surprise when his sister-in-law Mary, his older brother John's wife had become pregnant so soon after getting married. He had remarked *"My word Kate they haven't lost much time, have they?"* He may have felt trapped. Perhaps also after all that had happened to them over the previous five years, both Peter and Kate had changed. Life had taken them in different directions. It may be at this stage they did not recognise what the other had become.

After Peter's experience on the battlefield; the horrors he had witnessed and others that he had been responsible for, he may have been suffering from Post-Traumatic Stress Disorder, a condition not yet recognised in 1917. But loved ones, friends and family would experience the situation with a returning soldier in the phrase, "I see you, I feel you, but you are not here".

It is my opinion that Kate loved Peter. While in Blackpool Kate and Jean would have had time to reflect on their situations. Kate had left behind her job as Assistant Matron in Napier. Her hard work over the years had been recognised and rewarded. She may have been quite attached to the girls at the high school who boarded, attending to their needs, seeing them through joy and sorrow as they grew up in a time of war. I am sure she would have had a good rapport with their parents.

She had made many friends in New Zealand. She was relatively young and not unattractive so she would have received the interest of men with offers to settle there and start a family. For example there is the letter from Charles, who had moved to Australia asking her to be his partner.

She enjoyed the countryside and would have felt pleased that she had seen much of it on horseback. She had travelled around North Island, and experienced the depth of its natural beauty and its unique fascinations.

Yet she had given up all this to return home to be with Peter as she kept her promise to him. She had written almost every week to him over the five years they had been apart: over 200 letters! She was still writing to him in his convalescence. She was pregnant with his child. She needed to see him. They needed to discuss their future. Would he keep his promise to her?

Peter was being rehabilitated in Roehampton which was known as the Human Repair Factory. Soon after the War had started Mary Gwynne Holford, a society philanthropist, visited a Military Hospital and was distressed when she saw a soldier who had lost both his arms. In response she made plans for a hospital that would help mutilated war casualties and provide them with "the most perfect artificial limbs human science could devise".

With the help of friends and associates, she set about fundraising and the site of Roehampton House in south London was chosen. Built as a stately home in 1712, Roehampton House was purchased in 1915 by a shipping magnate, and placed at the disposal of the government for use during the War.

With Queen Mary's influence, the Queen Mary's Convalescent Auxiliary Hospital *(PC19A)* was opened on 28 June 1915 with 200 beds.

The demand for rehabilitation increased as casualties mounted. The Hospital responded by increasing its capacity; by the time Peter received treatment some 11,000 patients had already been treated there. Men fitted with prosthetic limbs learned how to walk again. They also learned other skills such as carpentry.

By November 1918 Roehampton had 900 beds and a waiting list of over 4000 patients. Of the 1.65 million men in the British Army that were wounded in the War, it is estimated that 240,000 of these suffered total or partial leg or arm amputations as a result of war wounds (Ref 19).

I am sure Peter would have been grateful for his treatment and that he was able to walk again; having recovered, he left Roehampton. He was going to see his old friend Bob Duffus; they had always talked

Kate in her wedding dress She does not appear to be very happy Peter and Kate were married in London 20 September 1917 (PC19B)

things through. He would also see Mrs D and find out what his factory in Lutterworth was doing for the war effort. He had been away a long time.

Wednesday night Lutterworth [Possibly 15 August 1917 *(Ref 6)*]
My Dearest Kate,

I have had two letters today from you and as you say I am still at the old address. I am not quite sure which day I go to London. It may be tomorrow or perhaps Saturday.

Anyhow whatever your arrangements are I should like to see you in London and by the time-table I see you can get a good train from Blackpool Central at 2.10 arriving Euston 8.45 P.M. I will meet you at Euston. You had better make it Tuesday. I will expect you then. What my arrangements are I am not sure but expect to go to Sheffield University soon.

Best wishes, Yours Peter

Rather a cool letter and very matter of fact. Not signed in his usual fashion *"with fondest love, your loving Peter".*

A month after this arranged meeting with Peter in London and with Kate six months pregnant they were married on 20 September 1917 in the Parish of St Stephen Bow London *(Ref 78)*. Kate's wedding and engagement rings survive (see front cover). She does not look very happy in her wedding dress *(PC19B)*. Things were not going well after her initial arrival in Britain and the happy reunion at Jimmie's wedding. Peter had changed. He left soon after the wedding. He did not help during the pregnancy and he was not present at the birth of his son.

20

1918 AND AFTER

On Friday 4 January 1918 Kate gave birth to Elliot Alexander Wardlaw at 97 Norville Street London. His birth was registered on 4 February 1918 in the Registration District of Poplar in the Sub-District of Bow in London *(PC20A)*. Peter was not present; he did not sign the Birth Certificate *(Ref 79)*. He is however recorded as the father - Peter Hutchinson Wardlaw, Lieutenant Royal Field Artillery (Mechanical Engineer).

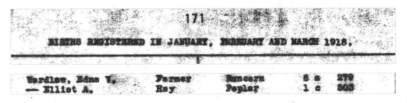

Record of Elliot Alexander Wardlaw's birth Poplar London 4 January 1918 (PC20A)

My father, Elliot Alexander Wardlaw, was not named after Peter, but after the little boy Elliot whom my Grandmother adored. She had been his Nanny when she worked for Mrs Lean in Glasgow. Elliot's middle name, Alexander, is in memory of Peter's youngest brother.

An item of News recorded in the Evening Standard on Monday 9 September 1918 States - "A Wife's Complaint. An officer's wife told the Highgate magistrates today that they were married last September. He went away immediately after the ceremony, but before going he promised to provide a home for her. He has not done so. She has only seen him once since, and he then ignored her. She was granted a summons for 'neglect to maintain'." *(PC20B)*

Peter had abandoned his wife and son.

A Wife's Complaint.

An officer's wife told the Highgate magistrates to-day that they were married last September. He went away immediately after the ceremony, but before going he promised to provide a home for her. He had not done so. She had only seen him once since, and he then ignored her. She was granted a summons for " neglect to maintain."

Complaint in the Evening Standard Monday 9 September 1918 Peter (the Officer) is accused of not providing for Kate and his Son (PC20B)

There is a certificate issued by the Local Authority, Borough of Hornsey in Greater London registering Catherine Wardlaw of 26 Elm Grove, Crouch End North for Household Duties under the National Registration Act of 1915 *(PC20C)*. So it is likely she remained in London and worked as a domestic servant supporting herself and her new born son *(PC20D)*.

There was a county court order to provide Kate with maintenance payments which I once had in my possession but has subsequently been lost.

Jean Kemp met a sailor in The Royal Navy called Frank Allan when in New Zealand where they were married. They eventually settled in Plymouth. As for Will Berry I do not know where his life had taken him.

The War finally ended on 11 November 1918. Had humanity come to its senses? Life carried on. Babies were born.

In December 1918 Jean sent a photo of herself and her four month

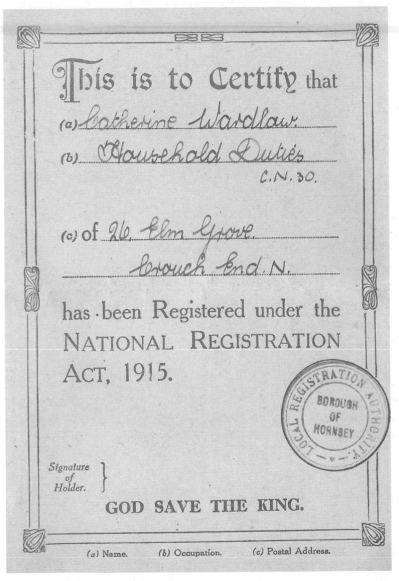

This is to Certify that

(a) *Catherine Wardlaw.*

(b) *Household Duties*

C.N. 30.

(c) of *26 Elm Grove.*

Crouch End. N.

has been Registered under the NATIONAL REGISTRATION ACT, 1915.

Signature of Holder. }

GOD SAVE THE KING.

LOCAL REGISTRATION AUTHORITY · BOROUGH OF HORNSEY

(a) Name. (b) Occupation. (c) Postal Address.

Kate remained in London working as a domestic servant after the birth of her son in 1918. She supported herself and her son (PC20C)

Kate with her son Elliot Alexander Wardlaw aged 3 months 1918 (PC20D)

old daughter to Kate stating "A wee Colonial wishes her Cousin Elliot a merry Xmas." *(PC20E & F)*

There is also a card dated Xmas 1919 from Miss Greig sending her

Jean with her daughter Jeannie aged four months Christmas 1918 (PC20E)

love and wishing Kate and wee Elliot a very happy Xmas *(PC20G)*. She signs it LB Greig, using the informal 'Lettie' instead of Violet. After parting three years ago they may have been missing one another's company. Unfortunately no letters survive.

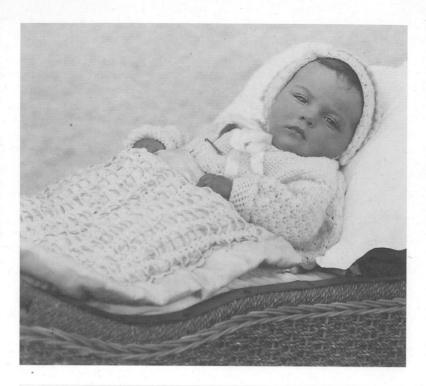

Baby Jeannie Allan Kemp (PC20F)

> A wee Colonial
> wishes Her wee
> Cousin Elliot
> A merry Xmas.
> Jean Allan Kemp
> Taken in her pram
> aged 4 months

(PC20F)

At some stage Kate moved from London back to Alloa, but eventually settled in Bo'ness on the South side of the River Forth sixteen miles from Alloa. There she ran a Grocer's shop where she brought up Elliot Wardlaw on her own *(PC20H-K)*. Peter played no part in my father's life as he grew up.

Elliot was all that Peter could give to Kate, by accident or otherwise. Perhaps as her son grew up she would see in his looks, his mannerisms and his behaviour something of her *"loving Peter"*.

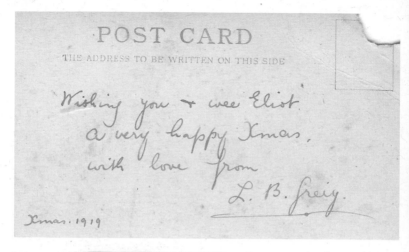

Christmas wishes from Miss Grieg Head Mistress at The Girls' School Napier (PC20G)

Kate with her son Elliot Alexander Wardlaw aged 1 (PC20H)

Kate with her son Elliot Alexander Wardlaw aged 2 (PC20I)

Kate with her son Elliot aged 14 happy times (PC20J)

Kate & Elliot ready for university 1936 (PC20K)

Peter was kept on by the Army under the Employment of the Ministry of Labour. He lived in London, but would keep close ties with Lutterworth, where presumably he continued to have a business interest. At some stage Peter started a relationship with Carrie Whiston who was born in Lutterworth in 1902. She was thirteen years younger than him and had married in 1926; records indicate that this took place in Islington London *(Ref 1)*.

Elliot Alexander Wardlaw *(PC20K)* went to Edinburgh University in 1936 to study Medicine. After he had completed his second year, he and some University friends went on holiday and he visited his Aunt Jean in Plymouth. Jean writes to Kate about this visit.

26. 8. 38. 3 Underhill Villas, Stoke, Plymouth.
My Dear Kate,

Just a wee note to tell you, we had Elliot and his friends to see us on Wednesday, and we thoroughly enjoyed their visit. There isn't a bit of difference in Elliot (except that he has grown up). Frank and I would have known him anywhere. Still the same nice quiet lad. Frank was asking him if he remembered his collection of chocolate fishes etc. that he had the last time we saw him more than 14 years ago.

We did like the Boyd family too; they are all so jolly and nice. It's lovely for Elliot to have such nice friends to go around with; he is just like one of themselves. I am sure it must be a great joy to you Kate to know he is in such good company. Much better than being off with young boys. I've no doubt you are very proud of him, and he is really well worth it Kate. But don't tell him I said so.

And how are you keeping yourself now. Better I hope. Elliot has promised me that he will try to persuade you to come down for a holiday with me whenever you feel fit to travel the long journey. I wish we were a bit nearer, but a good rest after the journey would do you worlds of good. Now, don't forget, we shall love to have you at any time Kate.

Meantime, see and take care of yourself. Please remember us to Rena and all her family when you see them. Much love from we three.

Yours very sincerely, Jean.

Was Jean reassuring Kate that in her son Elliot, it was all worthwhile? Was this remark to counter regrets that they had come back from their new life in New Zealand; or that there was a good outcome from her broken relationship with Peter? I will never know. My father did say that Kate never said a bad word about his father. He said, as she told him, that the War had changed him especially being buried alive and losing his leg. Would they have loved and lived together if he had not become a casualty? At Messines his luck ran out. He was torn apart both physically and emotionally. What they had hoped to share together had been broken.

When Jean wrote this letter she would not have known how bad Kate's health was *(PC20L)*. She was in the late stages of valvular heart disease, a consequence of the Rheumatic fever she had contracted while on the way to New Zealand on the SS Remuera. Her heart was failing. She died on 3 December 1938 *(Ref 80)*. My Father was always quite sad as the calendar approached December. He would recount to us how he had held her in his arms as she died; the only parent he had ever known.

Kate was buried in Sunnyside Cemetery Alloa *(PC20M & PC20N)*. After the service my Father was told by his uncle Jimmie that Peter had been at the cemetery in a black cab observing the graveside

Kate with a friend summer 1938 she was not well (PC20L)

service from a distance. Peter had excelled as a businessman, and as a military man why could he not be a husband and father even at this late moment?

He hid in his cab unable or unwilling to face his broken promise. And again he missed an opportunity to embrace his son.

Kate had left everything to her son *(PC20O)*. This Will was written on

No. 1100

SUNNYSIDE CEMETERY.

ALLOA 6 17 19 38

Mr Elliot A. Wardlaw

To Alloa Town Council Cemetery Committee.

To Fees of Interment of Kate L Wardlaw		aged 50	
in Lair No. 37 Section 10		£	1 : 13 : 9
„ Carriages entering Grounds,			:
„ Moving and Replacing Monumental Stone, etc.,			:
19	Received Payment,	£	1 : 13 : 9

A Gowan Clerk.

Kate died on 5 December 1938 and was buried in Sunnyside Cemetery Alloa (PC20M)

22 January 1931 just after Elliot's thirteenth birthday.

It is hard not to condemn Peter for turning away from his wife and son. Life changes people. We who have never lived through the gruesome sharp end of a battle front are in no position to judge. In my view there is a change in Peter's letters as he becomes hardened in the grip of all-consuming war. For example he seemed unable to grasp that Kate's desire to sail to the USA was her stating an intention to get back to Britain and fulfil their promises to one another.

It is even harder to understand why he never had any contact with his son. His brother Jimmie with his wife and children lived in Alloa and spent time with Kate and Elliot. My Father referred to him as Uncle Jimmie Wardlaw. Would Peter not have been aware of his son growing up? After Kate died could he have helped Elliot through Medical School? Perhaps he was never asked.

Elliot Wardlaw at his mother's grave aged 20 (PC20N)

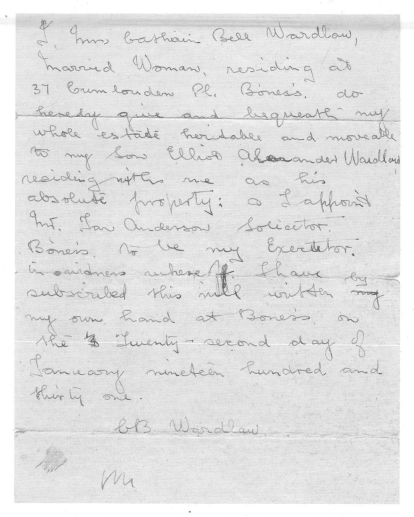

Kate's will written in January 1931 she left everything to her son Elliot he was 13 years old (PC20O)

Three months after the death of his wife Peter married Carrie Whiston in February 1939 in Chelsea, London *(Ref 1)*. I am sure my father was not aware of this event, as I think he would have told me.

What would Peter have thought when war was declared on Nazi Germany on 3 September 1939? All that sacrifice he had witnessed in "The War to end all Wars", was it for nothing? He was living in Hammersmith and working for the Civil Service in London. He would have experienced the Blitz between October 1940 and June 1941 as Hitler brought the war close to home. Four hundred and nineteen high explosive bombs were dropped on Hammersmith and Fulham causing immense destruction *(Ref 69)*.

Peter died suddenly on 3 July 1941 at Charing Cross Hospital London. He was only fifty three. The cause of death was not apparent. Such events then, as now, were presented to the Coroner to determine the cause of death.

A post-mortem examination revealed that Peter died from atheroma and thrombosis of the basilar artery in his brain *(Ref 81)*. The loss of blood supply to vital areas would have presented with a sudden and dramatic deterioration in brain function or more likely sudden death.

Sadly Peter never knew his son *(PC20P)* and I his grandson will never know why. However I do know so much more about my Grandparents and thank them for leaving me their story. It is beautifully ironic that it is Peter's letters that survive. He would often berate himself for not matching Kate's correspondence. Kate had treasured these letters, bringing them back with her when she returned to Scotland. She had kept them safe throughout her life. Perhaps for her they were the connection with happier times; of what might have been if Messines had not broken her *"loving Peter"*.

The Father and Son who never knew one another with the only parent Elliot ever knew; his Mother Kate. The family that never was (PC20P)

ADDENDUM

Elliot Alexander Wardlaw carried on with his studies at Medical School, but money was running out - he could not run a grocery business and meet the demands of third year medicine.

He didn't fulfil his dream of being a doctor. The Second World War was declared in 1939. Like his father had done, he enlisted and joined the Royal Air Force in another cruel War that would see him in Canada, Egypt and India.

It would be a long time before he met my mother.

LIST OF PICTURES

Chapter 1

Chapter 2

Chapter 3

Chapter 4

Chapter 5

Chapter 6

Chapter 7

No pictures

Chapter 8

Chapter 9

LIST OF MAPS

LIST OF CHAPTERS

ACKNOWLEDGMENTS

I would like to thank my wife Jane for putting up with me as I tackled this project. For her patience, her diligent correction of typographic errors, and numerous other suggestions. To my step-daughter Kirby for her help with anything on the computer outside my sphere of basic word processing.

To Dai Hughes my friend and neighbour for his professional expertise in designing the front cover, formatting and overall presentation of this book.

To Chris, and Michael my younger brothers, and Paul McNeilly my former colleague in General Practice for their helpful suggestions. To Alex Morgan for his photographs of the objects on the front cover. To Claire my sister-in-law for her 'Lusitania' photos.

I have attempted to extract the facts from my many references, and in so doing I have endeavoured to understand what my Grandparents lived through a hundred years ago. In acquiring facts I hope not to infringe on any copyright issues.

I apologise for any possible inaccuracies in my presentation but hope that none have been overlooked.

Above all I would like to thank the "Grandparents I never knew"; Kate for safely preserving these letters, and Peter for writing them even from the Battlefields of Gallipoli and The Somme so that I could have their story.

APPENDIX

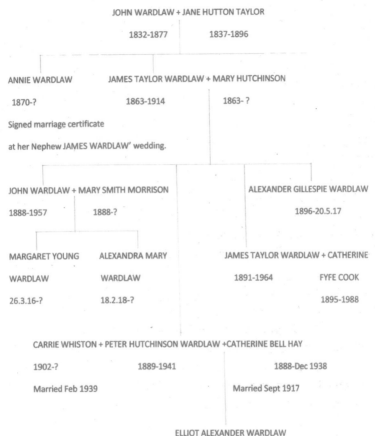

JOHN WARDLAW + JANE HUTTON TAYLOR

1832-1877   1837-1896

ANNIE WARDLAW   JAMES TAYLOR WARDLAW + MARY HUTCHINSON

1870-?   1863-1914   1863- ?

Signed marriage certificate

at her Nephew JAMES WARDLAW' wedding.

JOHN WARDLAW + MARY SMITH MORRISON   ALEXANDER GILLESPIE WARDLAW

1888-1957   1888-?   1896-20.5.17

MARGARET YOUNG   ALEXANDRA MARY   JAMES TAYLOR WARDLAW + CATHERINE

WARDLAW   WARDLAW   1891-1964   FYFE COOK

26.3.16-?   18.2.18-?   1895-1988

CARRIE WHISTON + PETER HUTCHINSON WARDLAW +CATHERINE BELL HAY

1902-?   1889-1941   1888-Dec 1938

Married Feb 1939   Married Sept 1917

ELLIOT ALEXANDER WARDLAW

4.1.1918-

1) Wardlaw Family Tree to 1918

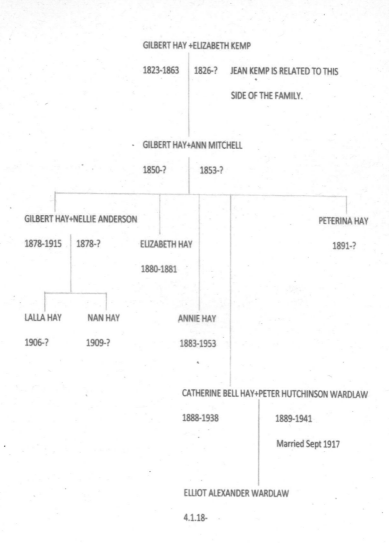

GILBERT HAY +ELIZABETH KEMP

1823-1863   1826-?   JEAN KEMP IS RELATED TO THIS

SIDE OF THE FAMILY.

GILBERT HAY+ANN MITCHELL

1850-?   1853-?

GILBERT HAY+NELLIE ANDERSON   PETERINA HAY

1878-1915   1878-?   ELIZABETH HAY   1891-?

1880-1881

LALLA HAY   NAN HAY   ANNIE HAY

1906-?   1909-?   1883-1953

CATHERINE BELL HAY+PETER HUTCHINSON WARDLAW

1888-1938   1889-1941

Married Sept 1917

ELLIOT ALEXANDER WARDLAW

4.1.18-

1) Hay Family Tree to 1918

REFERENCES

1. www.findmypast.co.uk
2. www.arthurlloyd.co.uk - *The Music Hall and Theatre History website*
3. www.grace'sguide.co.uk - *British Industrial History*
4. www.demtullpitcairn.com - *SS Remuera*
5. www.nghs.school.nz
6. ww.timeanddate.com
7. *"The First World War"* by John Keegan
8. *A Russian revelation; where the mythical Cossacks of WW1 were really from* - Telegraph article by Jasper Copping 23.2.2014
9. www.tudorrow.com - *Witley Military Camp*
10. www.vectorsite.net - *The First Battle of the Atlantic*
11. www.warpath.orbat.com - *11th (Northern) Division*
12. *"William and Lawrence Bragg, Father and Son"* by John Jenkin (p360-366)
13. *"Gallipoli"* by LA Carlyon
14. www.wikipedia.org - *IX Corps Gallipoli*
15. www.diggerhistory.info - *Orbats of Gallipoli Forces*
16. www.1914-1918.invisionzone.com - *Gallipoli - which ships carried 11th Division to Suvla?*
17. www.1914-1918.net - *Gallipoli*
18. www.1914-1918.net - *The Battle of Messines*
19. www.maryevans.com - *Repair factory at Roehampton*
20. www.wikepedia.org - *Military organisation*
21. *"The First World War"* by Peter Chasseaud. *The First World War through Maps from 1914 to 1918 (a) Gallipoli P.68-82. (b) The Battle of The Somme p172-187 (c) Battlefield Geometry p10-13 (d) Battle of Messines p228-230*
22. www.wikipedia.org - *HMS Paxton*
23. www.1914-1918. net - *What was an artillery brigade in 1914-1918?*
24. www.clydesite.co.uk -*RMS Remuera*
25. www.wikepedia.org - *What was an artillery brigade of the British Army*
26. www.battle-honours.eu - *LV111 Brigade of the Royal Field Artillery in 1914-1918*
27. www.widipedia.org - *Military divisions*
28. www.1914-1918.net — *Sir Ian Hamilton's Third Despatch*
29. www.gutenberg-e.org — *"The Infantry cannot do with a gun less" chapter 4 preparing the attack*
30. www.wartimememories.co.uk - *The Wartime Memories Project, 58 Brigade, Royal Field Artillery during the Great War*
31. www.longlongtrail.co.uk — *The history of the 11th (Northern) Division*

32.   www.wikipedia.org - *The Battle for Thiepval Ridge*

33.   *"Somme The Heroism and Horror of War"* By Martin Gilbert The first day of battle p50-90 The arrival of the tanks p183-191

34.   *"1915 - The Death of Innocence"* by Lyn Macdonald - Information re Gallipoli Campaign p343-455

35.   www.wikipedia.org - *Battle of Messines 1917*

36.   www.cargill.com

37.   www.wikepedia.org - *RMS Andania (1913)*

38.   www.maritimequest.com - *SS Andania*

39.   www.interactive.ancestry.co.uk - *UK Incoming Passenger Lists 1878-1960*

40.   *"New Zealand Lonely Planet Publications"* by P Harding, C Bain and Bedford

41.   www.nationalarchives.gov.uk - *British Army WW1 Medal Rolls Index Cards 1914 - 1920 for Peter H Wardlaw*

42.   *"The Face of Battle"* by John Keegan A Study of the Somme p204-336

43.   *"The Unknown Soldier"* by Neil Hanson

44.   *"The Sword bearers Studies in Supreme Command in the First World War"* by Correlli Barnett Part 111 General Petain p119-286

45.   *"Forgotten Voices of the Great War"* by Max Arthur 1916 p130-192, 1917 p194-247

46.   www.insightguides.com - *Family World Atlas*

47.   *"A Popular History of the Great War"* edited by Sir JJ Hammerton Vol 111 1916 (a) Somme Battles p195-259 (b) Battle of the Ancre p452-474 Vol 1V 1917 (c) French Offensive on the Aisne p174-191 (d) Battle of Messines Ridge p192-207

48.   *"The Mammoth Book of Modern Battles"* edited by Jon E Lewis Gallipoli (1915) by Nigel Bagnall p35-50

49.   www.nationalarchives.gov.uk - *Alexander Gillespie Wardlaw's war record British Army WW1 Rolls Index Cards*

50.   www.thisismoney.co.uk

51.   www.sandyhargove-collectorsnook.com - *Blackie's Children's Annuals*

52.   www.wikepedia.org - *The Gas Mantle*

53.   *The Woolworth Atlas of the World*

54.   *A Photo history of World War One* Philip J Hatthornthwaite (a) intro 1917 photo 23 (b) intro 1916 photo 27

55.   www.denniscorbett.com - *Search for your WW1 Gunner Ancestor*

56.   www.forces-war-records.com - *The 1914-1915 Star*

57.   www.military.rootweb.ancestory.com - *The Geography of the Great War*

58.   www.nzhistory.net.nz - *Horses stabled on Transport Ship*

59.   www.nzhistory.net.nz - *Escort ship Knight Templar*

60.   www.longlongtrail.co.uk - *The Royal Artillery in the First World War*

61. "A History of Medicine" Forwarded by Prof. Hero van Urk page 59 Published by Simon and Schuster

62. Registry of Births, Deaths and Marriages Alloa, Scotland

63. www.wikipedia.org - Alloa

64. Exterior View of Queen Mary's Convalescent Auxiliary Hospital in Roehampton showing main entrance and drive, 1914-18. From Red Cross archives. Image reference number 1447/IN2188

65. Googles Images - European Maps 1915

66. www.lamptech.co.uk - BTH Land at Leicester Road Rugby

67. www.lamptech.co.uk - BTH products

68. www.wikipedia.org - The Crystal Palace

69. www.bombsight.org - Blitz Hammersmith and Fulham, London

70. www.widipedia - North Island Main Trunk

71. "Standard of Power The Royal Navy in the Twentieth Century" by Dan Van Der Vat. Submarines p103-135

72. www.uboat.net - U-boat commanders

73. "The Scottish Regiments" Second Edition by Diana M. Henderson p153

74. "Doing Well and Doing Good: Ross and Glendining? Scottish Enterprise in New Zealand" by Stephen Jones Otago University Press

75. "Success in British History Since 1914" by Jack B Watson and John Murray Publishers Ltd p6 table 1.2

76. www.iexplore.com - Crossing the Drake Passage - A Survival Guide

77. www.vitoriaweb.org - Condolence letters spurred by the Penny Black, Catherine J Gordon Skidmore College

78. Peter and Kate's Marriage certificate

79. Elliot Alexander Wardlaw's birth certificate

80. Kate Wardlaw's death certificate

81. Peter Wardlaw's death certificate

82. www.rmslusitania.info - The Blue Riband

83. 1913 The World Before The Great War by Charles Emmerson p4